MEASURE,
For Measure.

In the same series

A PLEASANT CONCEITED HISTORIE, CALLED
THE TAMING OF A SHREW

THE TRAGICALL HISTORIE OF HAMLET PRINCE OF DENMARKE

THE CRONICLE HISTORY OF HENRY THE FIFT:
WITH HIS BATTELL FOUGHT AT AGIN COURT IN FRANCE
TOGETHER WITH AUNTIENT PISTOLL

AN EXCELLENT CONCEITED TRAGEDIE OF ROMEO AND JULIET

THE TRAGŒDY OF OTHELLO, THE MOORE OF VENICE

THE TRAGEDIE OF ANTHONIE, AND CLEOPATRA

THE MOST EXCELLENT HISTORIE OF
THE MERCHANT OF VENICE

TWELFE NIGHT, OR WHAT YOU WILL

M. WILLIAM SHAKE-SPEARE: HIS TRUE CHRONICLE HISTORY OF
THE LIFE AND DEATH OF KING LEAR
AND HIS THREE DAUGHTERS

THE TRAGEDIE OF JULIUS CÆSAR

THE TRAGEDY OF KING RICHARD THE THIRD

A MIDSOMMER NIGHTS DREAME

MEASURE, FOR MEASURE

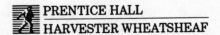
PRENTICE HALL
HARVESTER WHEATSHEAF

LONDON • NEW YORK • TORONTO • SYDNEY • TOKYO • SINGAPORE •
MADRID • MEXICO CITY • MUNICH

SHAKESPEAREAN ORIGINALS: FIRST EDITIONS

MEASURE, For Measure.

EDITED AND INTRODUCED BY
GRACE IOPPOLO

PRENTICE HALL

HARVESTER WHEATSHEAF

First published 1996 by
Prentice Hall Europe
Campus 400, Maylands Avenue
Hemel Hempstead
Hertfordshire, HP2 7EZ
A division of
Simon & Schuster International Group

Designed by Geoff Green

Typeset in 11pt Bembo
by Photoprint, Torquay, Devon

Printed and bound in Great Britain by
T.J. Press (Padstow) Ltd., Padstow, Cornwall

Library of Congress Cataloging-in-Publication Data

Shakespeare, William, 1564–1616.
    Measure for measure / by William Shakespeare ;
edited by Grace Ioppolo.
      p. cm. -- (Shakespearean originals)
    Includes bibliographical references.
    ISBN 0–13–355397–3
    I. Ioppolo, Grace, 1956– . II. Title. III. Series:
Shakespearean originals--first editions.
PR2750.B24 1996
822.3'3--dc20   96–2525
                                        CIP

British Library Cataloguing in Publication Data

A catalogue record for this book is available from
the British Library

ISBN 0–13–355397–3

---

1 2 3 4 5   00 99 98 97 96

Contents

General Introduction	I
Introduction	13
Select Bibliography	23
Textual History	25
TEXT: MEASURE, FOR MEASURE	27
Endnotes	III
Appendix: Photographic facsimiles	121

General Introduction

T H I S series puts into circulation single annotated editions of early modern play-texts whose literary and theatrical histories have been overshadowed by editorial practices dominant since the eighteenth century.

The vast majority of Shakespeare's modern readership encounters his works initially through the standard modernised editions of the major publishing houses, whose texts form the basis of innumerable playhouse productions and classroom discussions. While these textualisations vary considerably in terms of approach and detail, the overwhelming impression they foster is not of diversity but uniformity: the same plays are reprinted in virtually identical words, within a ubiquitous, standardised format. Cumulatively, such texts serve to constitute and define a particular model of Shakespeare's work, conjuring up a body of writing which is given and stable, handed down by the author like holy writ. But the canonical status of these received texts is ultimately dependent not upon a divine creator, but upon those editorial mediations (rendered transparent by the discursive authority of the very texts they ostensibly serve) that shape the manner in which Shakespeare's works are produced and reproduced within contemporary culture.

Many modern readers of Shakespeare, lulled by long-established editorial traditions into an implicit confidence in the object of their attention, probably have little idea of what a sixteenth-century printed play-text actually looked like. Confronted with an example, she or he could be forgiven for recoiling before the intimidating display of linguistic and visual strangeness – antique type, non-standardised spelling, archaic orthographic conventions, unfamiliar and irregular speech prefixes, oddly placed stage directions, and

[1]

possibly an absence of Act and scene divisions. 'It looks more like Chaucer than Shakespeare,' observed one student presented with a facsimile of an Elizabethan text, neatly calling attention to the peculiar elisions through which Shakespeare is accepted as modern, while Chaucer is categorised as ancient. A student reading Chaucer in a modern translation knows that the text is a contemporary version, not a historical document. But the modern translations of Shakespeare which almost universally pass as accurate and authentic representations of an original – the standard editions – offer themselves as simultaneously historical document and accessible modern version – like a tidily restored ancient building.

The earliest versions of Shakespeare's works existed in plural and contested forms. Some nineteen of those plays modern scholars now attribute to Shakespeare (together with the non-dramatic verse) appeared in cheap quarto format during his life, their theatrical provenance clearly marked by an emphasis upon the companies who owned and produced the plays rather than the author.[1] Where rival quartos of a play were printed, these could contrast starkly: the second quarto of *The tragicall historie of Hamlet, prince of Denmarke* (1604), for example, is almost double the length of its first quarto (1603) predecessor and renames many of the leading characters. In 1623, Shakespeare's colleagues Heminge and Condell brought out posthumously the prestigious and expensive First Folio, the earliest collected edition of his dramatic works. This included major works, such as *The Tragedy of Macbeth*, *The Tragedie of Anthonie, and Cleopater*, and *The Tempest*, which had never before been published. It also contained versions of those plays, with the exception of *Pericles*, which had earlier appeared in quarto, versions which in some cases differ so markedly from their notional predecessors for them to be regarded not simply as variants of a single work, but as discrete textualisations independently framed within a complex and diversified project of cultural production; perhaps, even, in some senses, as separate plays. In the case of *Hamlet*, for example, the Folio includes some eighty lines which are not to be found in the second quarto, yet omits a fragment of around 230 lines which includes Hamlet's final soliloquy,[2] and far greater differences exist between certain other pairings.

This relatively fluid textual situation continued throughout the

[2]

General Introduction

seventeenth century. Quartos of individual plays continued to appear sporadically, usually amended reprints of earlier editions, but occasionally introducing new works, such as the first publication of Shakespeare and Fletcher's *The two noble kinsmen* (1634), a play which was perhaps excluded from the Folio on the basis of its collaborative status.[3] The title of another work written in collaboration with Fletcher, *Cardenio*, was entered on the Stationer's Register of 1653, but it appears not to have been published and the play is now lost. The First Folio proved a commercial success and was reprinted in 1632, although again amended in detail. In 1663, a third edition appeared which in its 1664 reprinting assigned to Shakespeare seven plays, never before printed in folio, viz. *Pericles Prince of Tyre; The London prodigall; The history of Thomas Ld Cromwell; Sir John Oldcastle Lord Cobham; The Puritan widow; A Yorkshire tragedy; The tragedy of Locrine*. These attributions, moreover, were accepted uncritically by the 1685 Fourth Folio.

The assumptions underlying seventeenth-century editorial practice, particularly the emphasis that the latest edition corrects and subsumes all earlier editions, is rarely explicitly stated. They are graphically illustrated, though, by the Bodleian Library's decision to sell off as surplus to requirements the copy of the First Folio it had acquired in 1623 as soon as the enlarged 1663 edition came into its possession.[4] Eighteenth-century editors continued to work within this tradition. Rowe set his illustrated critical edition from the 1685 Fourth Folio, introducing further emendations and modernisations. Alexander Pope used Rowe as the basis of his own text, but he 'corrected' this liberally, partly on the basis of variants contained with the twenty-eight quartos he catalogued but more often relying on his own intuitive judgement, maintaining that he was merely 'restoring' Shakespeare to an original purity which had been lost through 'arbitrary Additions, Expunctions, Transpositions of scenes and lines, Confusions of Characters and Persons, wrong application of Speeches, corruptions of innumerable passages'[5] introduced by actors. Although eighteenth-century editors disagreed fiercely over the principles of their task, all of them concurred in finding corruption at every point of textual transmission (and in Capell's case, composition), and sought the restoration of a perceived poetic genius: for Theobald, Warburton, Johnson and Steevens,

General Introduction

'The multiple sources of corruption justified editorial intervention; in principle at least, the edition that had received the most editorial attention, the most recent edition, was the purest because the most purified.'[6]

This conception of the editorial function was decisively challenged in theory and practice by Edmund Malone, who substituted the principles of archaeology for those of evolution. For Malone, there could be only one role for an editor: to determine what Shakespeare himself had written. Those texts which were closest to Shakespeare in time were therefore the only true authority; the accretions from editorial interference in the years which followed the publication of the First Folio and early quartos had to be stripped away to recover the original. Authenticity, that is, was to be based on restoration understood not as improvement but as rediscovery. The methodology thus offered the possibility that the canon of Shakespeare's works could be established decisively, fixed for all time, by reference to objective, historical criteria. Henceforth, the text of Shakespeare was to be regarded, potentially, as monogenous, derived from a single source, rather than polygenous.

Malone's influence has proved decisive to the history of nineteenth- and twentieth-century bibliographic studies. Despite, however, the enormous growth in knowledge concerning the material processes of Elizabethan and Jacobean book production, the pursuit of Shakespeare's original words sanctioned a paradoxical distrust of precisely those early texts which Malone regarded as the touchstone of authenticity. Many assumed that these texts must themselves have been derived from some kind of authorial manuscript, and the possibility that Shakespeare's papers lay hidden somewhere exercised an insidious fascination upon the antiquarian imagination. Libraries were combed, lofts ransacked, and graves plundered, but the manuscripts have proved obstinately elusive, mute testimony to the low estimate an earlier culture had placed upon them once performance and publication had exhausted their commercial value.

Undeterred, scholars attempted to infer from the evidence of the early printed texts the nature of the manuscript which lay behind them. The fact that the various extant versions differed so considerably from each other posed a problem which could only be partially resolved by the designation of some as 'Bad Quartos', and therefore

[4]

non-Shakespearean; for even the remaining 'authorised' texts varied between themselves enormously, invariably in terms of detail and often in terms of substance. Recourse to the concept of manuscript authenticity could not resolve the difficulty, for such a manuscript simply does not exist.[7] Faced with apparent textual anarchy, editors sought solace in Platonic idealism: each variant was deemed an imperfect copy of a perfect (if unobtainable) paradigm. Once again, the editor's task was to restore a lost original purity, employing compositor study, collation, conflation and emendation.[8]

Compositor study attempts to identify the working practices of the individuals who set the early quartos and the Folio, and thus differentiate the non-Shakespearean interference, stripping the 'veil of print from a text' and thus attempting 'to recover a number of precise details of the underlying manuscript'.[9] Collation, the critical comparison of different states of a text with a view to establishing the perfect condition of a particular copy, provided systematic classification of textual variations which could be regarded as putative corruptions. Emendation allows the editor to select one of the variations thrown up by collation and impose it upon the reading of the selected control text, or where no previous reading appeared satisfactory, to introduce a correction based upon editorial judgement. Conflation is employed to resolve the larger scale divergences between texts, so that, for example, the Folio *Tragedie of Hamlet, Prince of Denmarke* is often employed as the control text for modern editions of the play, but since it 'lacks' entire passages found only in the second quarto, these are often grafted on to the former to create the fullest 'authoritative' text.

The cuts to the Folio *Hamlet* may reflect, however, not a corruption introduced in the process of transmission, but a deliberate alteration to the text authorised by the dramatist himself. In recent years, the proposition that Shakespeare revised his work and that texts might therefore exist in a variety of forms has attracted considerable support. The most publicised debate has centred on the relationship of the Quarto *M. William Shak-speare: his true chronicle historie of the life and death of King Lear and his three daughters* and the Folio *Tragedie of King Lear*.[10] The editors of the recent Oxford Shakespeare have broken new ground by including both texts in their one-volume edition on the grounds that the *Tragedie* represents an authorial revision of the earlier *Historie*, which is sufficiently radical to justify classifying it as a separate play. Wells and Taylor founded their revisionist position upon a recognition of the fact that Shakespeare was primarily a working *dramatist* rather than literary author and that he addressed his play-texts towards a particular audience of theatrical professionals who were expected to flesh out the bare skeleton of the performance script: 'The written text of any such manuscript thus depended upon an unwritten para-text which always accompanied it: an invisible life-support system of stage directions, which Shakespeare could expect his first audience to supply, or which those first readers would expect Shakespeare himself to supply orally.'[11] They are thus more open than many of their predecessors to the possibility that texts reflect their theatrical provenance and therefore that a plurality of authorised texts may exist, at least for certain of the plays.[12] They remain, however, firmly author centred – the invisible life-support system can ultimately always be traced back to the dramatist himself and the plays remain under his parental authority.[13]

What, however, if it were not Shakespeare but the actor Burbage who suggested, or perhaps insisted on, the cuts to *Hamlet*? Would the Folio version of the play become unShakespearean? How would we react if we *knew* that the Clown spoke 'More than is set down' and that his ad libs were recorded? Or that the King's Men sanctioned additions by another dramatist for a Court performance? Or that a particular text recorded not the literary script of a play but its performance script? Of course, in one sense we cannot know these things. But drama, by its very nature, is overdetermined, the product of multiple influences simultaneously operating across a single site of cultural production. Eyewitness accounts of performances of the period suggest something of the provisionality of the scripts Shakespeare provided to his theatrical colleagues:

> After dinner on the 21st of september, at about two o'clock, I went with my companions over the water, and in the thatched playhouse saw the tragedy of the first Emperor Julius with at least fifteen characters very well acted. At the end of the comedy they danced according to their custom with extreme elegance. Two in men's clothes and two in women's gave this performance, in wonderful combination with each other.[14]

[6]

General Introduction

This passage offers what can seem a bizarre range of codes; the thatched playhouse, well-acted tragedy, comic aftermath and elegant transvestite dance, hardly correspond to the typology of Shakespearean drama our own culture has appropriated. The Swiss tourist Thomas Platter was in fact fortunate to catch the curious custom of the jig between Caesar and the boy dressed as Caesar's wife, for by 1612 'all Jigs, Rhymes and Dances' after plays had been 'utterly abolished' to prevent 'tumults and outrages whereby His Majesty's Peace is often broke'.[15] Shakespeare, however, is the 'author' of the spectacle Platter witnessed only in an extremely limited sense; in this context the dramatist's surname functions not simply to authenticate a literary masterpiece, but serves as a convenient if misleading shorthand term alluding to the complex material practices of the Elizabethan and Jacobean theatre industry.[16] It is in the latter sense that the term is used in this series.

Modern theoretical perspectives have destabilised the notion of the author as transcendent subject operating outside history and culture. This concept is in any event peculiarly inappropriate when applied to popular drama of the period. It is quite possible that, as Terence Hawkes argues, 'The notion of a single "authoritative" text, immediately expressive of the plenitude of its author's mind and meaning, would have been unfamiliar to Shakespeare, involved as he was in the collaborative enterprise of dramatic production and notoriously unconcerned to preserve in stable form the texts of most of his plays.'[17] The script is, of course, an integral element of drama, but it is by no means the only one. This is obvious in forms of representation, such as film, dependent on technologies which emphasise the role of the *auteur* at the expense of that of the writer. But even in the early modern theatre, dramatic realisation depended not just upon the scriptwriter,[18] but upon actors, entrepreneurs, promptbook keepers, audiences, patrons, etc.; in fact, the entire wide range of professional and institutional interests constituting the theatre industry of the period.

Just as the scriptwriter cannot be privileged over all other influences, nor can any single script. It is becoming clear that within Elizabethan and Jacobean culture, around each 'Shakespeare' play there circulated a wide variety of texts, performing different theatrical functions and adopting different shapes in different contexts of production. Any of these contexts may be of interest to the modern reader. The so-called Bad Quartos, for example, are generally marginalised as piratically published versions based upon the memorial reconstructions of the plays by bit-part actors. But even if the theory of memorial reconstruction is correct (and it is considerably more controversial than is generally recognised[19]), these quarto texts would provide a unique window on to the plays as they were originally performed and open up exciting opportunities for contemporary performance.[20] They form part, that is, of a rich diversity of textual variation which is shrouded by those traditional editorial practices which have sought to impose a single, 'ideal' paradigm.

In this series we have sought to build upon the pioneering work of Wells and Taylor, albeit along quite different lines. They argue, for example, that

> The lost manuscripts of Shakespeare's work are not the fiction of an idealist critic, but particular material objects which happen at a particular time to have existed, and at another particular time to have been lost, or to have ceased to exist. Emendation does not seek to construct an ideal text, but rather to restore certain features of a lost material object (that manuscript) by correcting certain apparent deficiencies in a second material object (this printed text) which purports to be a copy of the first. Most readers will find this procedure reasonable enough.[21]

The important emphasis here is on the relative status of the two forms, manuscript and printed text: the object of which we can have direct knowledge, the printed text, is judged to be corrupt by conjectural reference to the object of which we can by definition have no direct knowledge, the uncorrupted (but non-existent) manuscript. This corresponds to no philosophical materialism we have encountered. The editors of *Shakespearean Originals* reject the claim that it is possible to construct a rehabilitated text reflecting a form approximating Shakespeare's artistic vision.[22] Instead we prefer to embrace the early printed texts as authentic material objects, the concrete forms from which all subsequent editions ultimately derive.

We therefore present within this series particular textualisations of plays which are not necessarily canonical or indeed even written by *William Shakespeare, Gent*, in the traditional sense; but which nevertheless represent important facets of Shakespearean drama. In the same way that we have rejected the underlying principles of traditional editorial practice, we have also approached traditional editorial procedures with extreme caution, preferring to let the texts speak for themselves with a minimum of editorial mediation. We refuse to allow speculative judgements concerning the exact contribution of the various individuals involved in the production of a given text the authority to license alterations to that text, and as a result relegate compositor study and collation[23] to the textual apparatus rather than attempt to incorporate them into the text itself through emendation.

It seems to us that there is in fact no philosophical justification for emendation, which foregrounds the editor at the expense of the text. The distortions introduced by this process are all too readily incorporated into the text as holy writ. Macbeth's famous lines, for example, 'I dare do all that may become a man, / Who dares do more, is none,' on closer inspection turn out to be Rowe's. The Folio reads, 'I dare do all that may become a man, / Who dares no more is none.' There seems to us no pressing reason whatsoever to alter these lines,[24] and we prefer to confine all such editorial speculation to the critical apparatus. The worst form of emendation is conflation. It is now widely recognised that the texts of the *M. William Shake-speare: his true chronicle historie of King Lear and his three daughters* (1608) and *The Tragedie of King Lear* (1623) differ so markedly that they must be considered as two distinct plays and that the composite *King Lear* which is reproduced in every twentieth-century popular edition of the play is a hybrid which grossly distorts both the originals from which it is derived. We believe that the case of *Lear* is a particularly clear example of a general proposition: that *whenever* distinct textualisations are conflated, the result is a hybrid without independent value. It should therefore go without saying that all the texts in this series are based upon single sources.

The most difficult editorial decisions we have had to face concern the modernisation of these texts. In some senses we have embarked upon a project of textual archaeology and the logic of our position points towards facsimile editions. These, however, are already available in specialist libraries, where they are there marginalised by

General Introduction

those processes of cultural change which have rendered them alien and forbidding. Since we wish to challenge the hegemony of standard editions by circulating the texts within this series as widely as possible, we have aimed at 'diplomatic' rather than facsimile status and have modernised those orthographic and printing conventions (such as long s, positional variants of u and v, i and j, ligatures and contractions) which are no longer current and likely to confuse. We do so, however, with some misgiving, recognising that as a result certain possibilities open to the Elizabethan reader are thereby foreclosed. On the other hand, we make no attempt to standardise such features as speech prefixes and *dramatis personae*, or impose conventions derived from naturalism, such as scene divisions and locations, upon the essentially fluid and non-naturalistic medium of the Elizabethan theatre. In order that our own editorial practice should be as open as possible we provide as an appendix a sample of the original text in photographic facsimile.

GRAHAM HOLDERNESS AND BRYAN LOUGHREY

NOTES AND REFERENCES

1. The title page of the popular *Titus Andronicus*, for example, merely records that it was 'Plaide by the Right Honourable the Earle of Darbie, Earle of Pembrooke, and Earle of Sussex their Servants', and not until 1598 was Shakespeare's name attached to a printed version of one of his plays, *Love's Labour's Lost*.
2. For a stimulating discussion of the relationship between the three texts of *Hamlet*, see Steven Urkowitz, ' "Well-sayd olde Mole", Burying Three *Hamlets* in Modern Editions', in Georgianna Ziegler (ed.), *Shakespeare Study Today* (New York: AMS Press, 1986), pp. 37–70.
3. In the year of Shakespeare's death Ben Jonson staked a far higher claim for the status of the playwright, bringing out the first ever collected edition of English dramatic texts, *The Workes of Beniamin Jonson*, a carefully prepared and expensively produced folio volume. The text of his Roman tragedy *Sejanus*, a play originally written with an unknown collaborator, was carefully revised to preserve the purity of authorial input. See Bryan Loughrey and Graham Holderness, 'Shakespearean Features', in Jean Marsden (ed.), *The Appropriation of Shakespeare: Post-Renaissance Reconstructions of the Works and the Myth* (Hemel Hempstead: Harvester Wheatsheaf, 1991), p. 183.

General Introduction

4. F. Madan and G.M.R. Turbutt (eds), *The Original Bodleian Copy of the First Folio of Shakespeare* (Oxford: Oxford University Press, 1905), p. 5.

5. Cited in D. Nicol Smith, *Eighteenth Century Essays* (Oxford: Oxford University Press, 1963), p. 48.

6. Margreta de Grazia, *Shakespeare Verbatim* (Oxford: Oxford University Press, 1991), p. 62. De Grazia provides the fullest and most stimulating account of the important theoretical issues raised by eighteenth-century editorial practice.

7. Unless the Hand D fragment of 'The Booke of Sir Thomas Moore' (British Library Harleian MS 7368) really is that of Shakespeare. See Stanley Wells and Gary Taylor, *William Shakespeare: A Textual Companion* (Oxford: Oxford University Press, 1987), pp. 461–7.

8. See Margreta de Grazia, 'The Essential Shakespeare and the Material Book', *Textual Practice*, vol. 2, no. 1 (Spring 1988).

9. Fredson Bowers, 'Textual Criticism', in O.J. Campbell and E.G. Quinn (eds), *The Reader's Encyclopedia of Shakespeare* (New York: Methuen, 1966), p. 869.

10. See, for example, Gary Taylor and Michael Warren (eds), *The Division of the Kingdoms* (Oxford: Oxford University Press, 1983).

11. Stanley Wells and Gary Taylor, *William Shakespeare: A Textual Companion* (Oxford: Oxford University Press, 1987), p. 2.

12. See, for example, Stanley Wells, 'Plural Shakespeare', *Critical Survey*, vol. 1, no. 1 (Spring 1989).

13. See, for example, *Textual Companion*, p. 69.

14. Thomas Platter, a Swiss physician who visited London in 1599 and recorded his playgoing; cited in *The Reader's Encyclopaedia*, p. 634. For a discussion of this passage see Richard Wilson, *Julius Caesar: A Critical Study* (Harmondsworth: Penguin, 1992), chapter 3.

15. E.K. Chambers, *The Elizabethan Stage* (Oxford: Oxford University Press, 1923), pp. 340–1.

16. The texts of the plays sometimes encode the kind of stage business Platter recorded. The epilogue of *2 Henry IV*, for example, is spoken by a dancer who announces that 'My tongue is weary; when my legs are too, I will bid you good night . . .'

17. Terence Hawkes, *That Shakespeherian Rag* (London: Methuen, 1986), p. 75.

18. For a discussion of Shakespeare's texts as dramatic scripts, see Jonathan Bate, 'Shakespeare's Tragedies as Working Scripts', *Critical Survey*, vol. 3, no. 2 (1991), pp. 118–27.

19. See, for example, Random Cloud [Randall McLeod], 'The Marriage of

Good and Bad Quartos', *Shakespeare Quarterly*, vol. 33, no. 4 (1982), pp. 421–30.

20. See, for example, Bryan Loughrey, 'Q1 in Modern Performance', in Tom Clayton (ed.), *The 'Hamlet' First Published* (Newark: University of Delaware Press, 1992) and Nicholas Shrimpton, 'Shakespeare Performances in London and Stratford-Upon-Avon, 1984–5', *Shakespeare Survey* 39, pp. 193–7.

21. *Textual Companion*, p. 60.

22. The concept of authorial intention, which has generated so much debate amongst critics, remains curiously unexamined within the field of textual studies.

23. Charlton Hinman's Norton Facsimile of *The First Folio of Shakespeare* offers a striking illustration of why this should be so. Hinman set out to reproduce the text of the original First Folio, but his collation of the Folger Library's numerous copies demonstrated that 'every copy of the finished book shows a mixture of early and late states of the text that is peculiar to it alone'. He therefore selected from the various editions those pages he believed represented the printer's final intentions and bound these together to produce something which 'has hitherto been only a theoretical entity, an abstraction: *the* First Folio'. Thus the technology which would have allowed him to produce a literal facsimile in fact is deployed to create an ahistorical composite which differs in substance from every single original upon which it is based. See Charlton Hinman, *The First Folio of Shakespeare* (New York, 1968), pp. xxiii–xxiv.

24. Once the process begins, it becomes impossible to adjudicate between rival conjectural emendations. In this case, for example, Hunter's suggestion that Lady Macbeth should be given the second of these lines seems to us neither more nor less persuasive than Rowe's.

Introduction

THE first record of a performance of *Measure for Measure*, before King James I at Whitehall Palace, is noted in the Master of the Revels accounts for 26 December 1604:

By his Ma^tis On St Stiuens night in the
plaiers: Hall A play Caled Mesur
             for Mesur

According to J.W. Lever, the play was probably written 'between May and August 1604. The theatres, closed throughout 1603 on account of the plague, re-opened on 9 April 1604; and the play was probably performed for the first time in the summer months of that year' at the Globe Theatre. What happened to the play between its first appearance on stage in 1604 and its first appearance in print in the 1623 First Folio has been the source of much editorial speculation and controversy. Edmond Malone, one of Shakespeare's earliest, and best, editors, taught us in 1790 that 'the two great duties of an editor are, to exhibit the genuine text of his author, and to explain his obscurities'. Unfortunately, editors of *Measure for Measure* have become much too preoccupied with the second part of Malone's advice and with Dr Johnson's exaggerated complaint that 'there is perhaps not one of Shakespeare's plays more darkened than this, by the peculiarities of its author, and the unskilfulness of its editors, by distortions of phrase or negligence of transcription'.

The Folio text of *Measure for Measure*, contrary to Dr Johnson's assertion, is neither 'darkened' nor 'peculiar' nor 'distorted', and, in fact, its textual situation is much less complex than those of such plays as *Hamlet*, *King Lear*, or even *Troilus and Cressida*. Yet Johnson and his succeeding, and preceding, editors have so focused on the play's minor 'obscurities' that their quests for the ideal 'genuine text' have produced extravagant explanations for and theories of Shakespearean incompetence and non-Shakespearean interference in the text as it appears in the Folio. To this editor, the play seems wholly Shakespearean and possesses a textual integrity that should be respected; as one of Shakespeare's most thematically complex plays, it depends upon a complex textual foundation for support. Rather than requiring explanations of how and why it deviates from the 'genuine' text, and rather than requiring theories to rebuild it into that ideal text which probably never existed, the 1623 Folio text of *Measure for Measure* should be accepted as a printed version of the play as it existed in its Shakespearean form.

This Shakespearean form contains the type of inconsistencies, false starts, spare, literary stage directions (rather than precise, theatrical ones) and duplications of speeches and actions characteristic of plays printed from Shakespeare's 'foul papers', yet the text also contains the formal act–scene divisions and spellings found in the transcripts of the King's Men's scribe of the 1620s, Ralph Crane. Other idiosyncrasies appear to suggest that the text at some distance may derive from a theatrical manuscript, perhaps a prompt-book. In addition, the compositors who set the type added their own characteristic marks to the text of the play. Thus, *Measure for Measure*'s previous editors' search for the 'genuine text' has led them to divide Shakespeare's contributions to the play from those of his scribe, his acting company, and his printers, even though such a division strips the play of its integrity and removes it from the collaborative theatrical process through which it passed. For these editors, the most pressing set of variables which produced the 'obscurities' in this text concerns what type of manuscript served as copy for the Folio compositors, for the 'authority' of this manuscript helps determine the text's closeness or distance from Shakespeare's original, authoritative draft. Most modern editors agree that the printer's copy was a manuscript copied out by Ralph Crane, who prepared transcripts of King's Men's plays from about 1619–25; what Ralph Crane was copying from is still in question.

Crane's copy could have been Shakespeare's 'foul papers', that is, his first complete draft of the play, which probably contained revisions, such as additions, cuts or corrections, made *currente calamo*, i.e. during composition, or at any period later from a few days to many years. This foul paper text may reflect an author quickly thrashing out a text without bothering to go back to correct errors or inconsistencies, or a deliberate author who returned to the text too much – that is, he made numerous revisions in character, plot, dialogue and structure (such revisions were often made in the margin of a manuscript or on inserted slips of paper; any of these revisions could be easily overlooked or misconstrued by the next person, whether scribe or compositor, who handled the foul papers). Besides foul papers, Crane may have been copying from a later transcript of some type of manuscript. Because a theatre company was required to submit a legible transcript of a play to the Master of the Revels for his inspection and licensing, the company often employed a scribe to make a 'fair copy' of the author's foul papers (some authors, including Shakespeare, may have made their own fair copies). This copy was usually later used to prepare a theatrical 'book' or master prompt-book (the licensed transcript may have been considered to be too valuable to use for performance; the foul papers remained the property of the acting company). Thus, alterations, cuts, additions, and/or errors and inconsistencies could be introduced into the text through the scribe's copying or the acting company's needs in staging the play (changes over time in acting personnel or venues induced alterations to a text). As with authorial changes, these changes could be made during the first performance of the play or some months or years later when the play was revived. In some cases, other dramatists, rather than the original author, made these changes or adapted the play. Thus Crane may have been copying from an authorial or scribal 'fair copy' or the company's prompt-book, or even a transcript of one of these manuscripts.

The type of manuscript finally submitted to compositors varied; although the King's Men apparently prepared intermediate transcripts for the printing of some plays in the Folio, such as *Measure for Measure*, other Folio texts, including *All's Well that Ends Well*, were printed directly from foul papers, and still other plays, which had already been printed in cheap quarto texts, were assembled from a collection of sources such as corrected quartos checked against a manuscript, as in the case, perhaps, of Folio *King Lear*.

Introduction

The compositors who set the type for the play can also be held responsible for errors and sometimes for deliberate alterations. Although most compositors seemed to work carefully and conservatively, some clearly made errors, especially when confronted by a manuscript that was difficult to decipher due to alterations such as cuts or additions (cuts, for example, were often marked with a simple vertical line drawn in the margin; such a mark could easily be overlooked).

Shakespeare's editors have thus catalogued 'obscurities' in the text of *Measure for Measure* deriving from these three stages of its transmission: its original composition (and possible later revision) by Shakespeare; its theatrical presentation by the King's Men from 1604 to 1622, and its preparation for and inclusion in the printing of the First Folio. One layer of obscurities appears to arise from its composition and includes the inconsistencies in the themes, content, characters and structure of the play. The text contains the types of Shakespearean markers that suggest it derives from his foul papers (other texts considered to be printed directly or indirectly from foul papers sharing the same characteristics include Quarto 1 of *Love's Labour's Lost* and Folio *Julius Caesar*). In particular, we see here Shakespeare's typical use of generic speech-prefixes for characters, even though they have character names (for example, Pompey is termed 'Clowne' in the speech-prefixes but is called by name in the dialogue). The 'false starts' include ghost or near-ghost characters, that is, characters Shakespeare included early in a stage direction or dialogue but for whom he provides little or no dialogue such as Varrius and the Justice (Juliet who remains silent in Act 1 Scene 3 does not, contrary to some arguments, appear to be a ghost character, but serves as a visible, pregnant symbol of the results of sexual intercourse that Angelo intends to ban). Other characters are confused: for example, Shakespeare presents a Friar Peter in Acts 4 and 5 who may or may not be the Friar Thomas who appears in Act 1. Minor inconsistencies appear in the play's time scheme: for example, the length of time cited for the Duke's failure to enforce the anti-fornication laws appears first as 19 years and later as 14 years, and the Duke seems confused throughout Act 4 as to how long it will take him to tie together all the parts of his plan to bring Angelo to justice. Some speeches in the play, particularly of the

Introduction

Duke in the opening speech in Act 1 Scene 1 and in his speech during Isabella and Mariana's private discussion in Act 4 Scene 1, appear to have missing or cut lines, resulting in confusion. Also, many exit markers are missing for characters who leave the stage and then re-enter; such missing stage directions nearly always derive from a composing author and not a playhouse scribe or bookkeeper who was responsible for the accuracy of the prompt-book.

The most notable set of 'obscurities' are a series of duplications (sometimes called 'repetition-brackets' by textual scholars), particularly in Act 1 Scene 2. When the Bawd, Mistress Over-don, appears on stage, she informs Lucio and the two Gentlemen that Claudio has been arrested for 'getting Madam *Julietta* with childe'. After the men leave the stage, Pompey, the Clown, appears and informs Over-don that 'Yonder man is carried to prison'. The Bawd appears surprised and questions Pompey, particularly about the new enforcement of the anti-fornication laws. Many scholars have cited this scene as a duplication, that is, a repetition of the information provided earlier at the Bawd's entrance; these scholars then debate whether the first or second discussion of Claudio's arrest was the first passage Shakespeare wrote. It is possible that Shakespeare rewrote the scene, intending to cancel one of the two discussions (many scholars assume the second passage was written first, largely because it is 'more Shakespearean', i.e. better dramatically); it is equally possible and more probable that Shakespeare did not immediately notice that he had produced a duplication (such authorial duplications also appear in Brutus' speeches in Act 4 Scene 3 on the death of Portia in *Julius Caesar* and Berowne's long speech in Act 4 Scene 3 on the Platonic image of women in *Love's Labour's Lost*). In fact, the duplication may be intentional; after all, Pompey does not name Claudio as the man carried to prison, and the Bawd's inquiry introduces a bawdy and witty dialogue on the results of the newly outlawed 'Groping for Trowts, in a peculiar River' and on their joint profession of proprietors of 'howses in the Suburbs'. In performance, this and other inconsistencies are not recognisable to an audience, but to editors, eager to present only a genuine text for which Shakespeare only should be held responsible, the inconsistencies must be explained as deriving from a non-Shakespearean source, lest Shakespeare be seen as a deficient dramatist. Yet as T.H. Howard-Hill has noted of this first printing of *Measure for Measure*, 'its principal textual deficiencies and inconsistencies are not of the kind for which compositors or scribe should be held responsible'. What these inconsistencies show us is not a deficient dramatist, but a dramatist at work, working and reworking his text, a pattern Shakespeare, as a revising author, employed in many of his other plays.

Nor should Ralph Crane's contributions to the final state of the text be seen as destructive or deficient. Although his transcript of *Measure for Measure* no longer exists, copies of his other transcripts, including Thomas Middleton's plays *The Witch* and *A Game at Chess*, demonstrate the ways in which he altered a text grammatically but not dramatically. As apparent in *Measure for Measure*, he hyphenated compound words, routinely used apostrophes, colons and parentheses, regularised speech-prefixes and act–scene divisions, made elisions, and repeated unusual spellings; in other words, Crane made significant grammatical corrections, but he did not alter dialogue, theme, character or structure, except possibly in editing out profanity. The text has been purged of oaths (especially 'God', probably as a result of the 1606 Act against profanity on the stage), at first suggesting that Crane's copy displayed some 1606 or later theatrical emendations to the text. However, Crane himself may have expurgated his transcript, as the three other Folio texts for which he prepared printers' copy (*The Tempest*, *The Two Gentlemen of Verona*, and *The Merry Wives of Windsor*) also lack profanity. The only addition in *Measure for Measure* for which he may be held responsible is the final cast list (which contains the only mention of the Duke's name as 'Vincentio'), which resembles others he prepared for Folio plays. As T.H. Howard-Hill has stated, 'the evidence of Crane's share in the preparation of copy for *MM* is ample enough'.

In addition to this scribal influence, bibliographers, including Howard-Hill, Charlton Hinman and Paul Werstine, have demonstrated that at least two of the four compositors who set the text of *Measure for Measure* introduced errors; also, in some sections, type was squeezed in or stretched due to miscalculations of 'casting-off' (the necessity of the printer counting off lines in a manuscript in order to determine on what page those lines would ultimately appéar). Some editors, including J.W. Lever and Brian Gibbons, have argued that the areas of squeezed or stretched type may indicate that the caster-off realised that certain passages in Crane's transcript were marked for deletion or addition and made adjustments which the final compositor did not recognise. However, Crane's other extant transcripts do not indicate that he would transcribe a deleted passage and then mark it for deletion; nor did he insert additions on extra sheets. Crane appears to have been very careful in his preparation of a manuscript, transcribing it as a finished, complete and coherent text without marking passages for deletion or addition, having made those changes already in the process of copying it out. Numerous lines in *Measure for Measure* are mislineated, others are prose lines printed as verse, possibly due to compositorial error, but also possibly due to Shakespeare's and/or Crane's uncertain or uncorrected presentation of the end or beginning of lines (extant authorial and scribal manuscripts of this age often show mislineation and prose–verse confusions).

Thus the nature of the copy from which Ralph Crane worked has been central in understanding the provenance of the Folio text of *Measure for Measure*, and its layers of non-authorial 'interference' and 'corruption' could explain why the play seemed to possess the 'peculiarities' of which Dr Johnson complained. J. Dover Wilson's contention that the text had been printed in 1623 from 'assembled' actors' 'parts' (actors were given only their own lines and their cues) set the stage for much of the twentieth-century preoccupation with the corruptions of the printed text. Wilson cited evidence of abridgement and expansion as well as two separate time schemes coexisting in the play, and he postulated that the play was first abridged in 1604 and was revised again through expansion by another dramatist to fit it once more for 'the common stage'. His conclusion about the transmission of the text depended on so many unsupported variables that it could not help but collapse:

> If we imagine that the abridgment of 1604 was made from the existing players' parts and not on Shakespeare's MS, that this original unabridged MS was afterwards lost, and that the prose adapter, therefore, constructed his text from the players' parts of 1604, hastily transcribing them and filling out the play with

additions of his own, we are making a not unreasonable guess as to the origin of the actual copy used for the printing of *Measure for Measure* as we now have it.

Wilson also argued that the text lacked integrity and contained remnants of an earlier non-Shakespearean play due to the presence of 'verse-fossils'. Such a theory was easily attacked by E.K. Chambers, who fought what he considered to be 'disintegration' of Shakespearean texts in assigning them to previous authors, and by W.W. Greg who pointed instead to F.P. Wilson's contention (later bolstered by Howard-Hill) that Ralph Crane produced some of the idiosyncrasies that Wilson used as evidence of 'assembling' and non-Shakespearean authorship. Greg more sensibly concluded that the play's inconsistencies 'may point to cutting or revision, or it may point to a hasty disregard of economy that more careful construction would have avoided'. Such economy convinced him that the scribe's copy was indeed 'foul papers that had been left in a rather rough state'.

Greg's theory that Crane was copying from Shakespeare's foul papers has been accepted by most modern editors, including Gibbons and N.W. Bawcutt (G.B. Evans acknowledged that it was equally possible that Crane was copying from a prompt-book). Yet Gary Taylor and John Jowett recently returned to J. Dover Wilson's theory that *Measure for Measure* was adapted by a dramatist other than Shakespeare. Taylor and Jowett claim that Crane's copy was the prompt-book, and they cite 'five emendations' in the text as evidence that Middleton and possibly John Webster adapted the play in 1621. They argue that the adapters (i) added the dialogue in Act 4 Scene 1 from the beginning of the scene until Mariana's first exit 24 lines later, also inserting the first stanza of a song which appears in a late 1610s King's Men's play, *Rollo, Duke of Normandy, or, The Bloody Brother*; (ii) transposed two of the Duke's soliloquies in Act 3 Scene 1 ('He who the sword of Heaven will beare . . . And performe an olde contracting') and Act 4 Scene 1 ('Oh Place, and greatnes: millions of false eies . . . And rack thee in their fancies') (a similar argument was proposed by William Warburton in 1747); (iii) added Act 1 Scene 2 from the beginning of the scene to the entrance of the Clowne; (iv) altered the first stage direction in Act 1 Scene 3 and following dialogue; (v) deleted 'Julietta' from the stage direction late in Act 5 Scene 1. Taylor and Jowett's arguments, although extremely interesting, depend upon too much unsupported speculation to be conclusive. To begin with, they cannot prove that Middleton wrote the long section of Act 1 Scene 2 and admit that it could be Shakespearean; many of their arguments, especially about Act 1 Scene 2, rest on topical allusions which they take to represent 1621 rather than 1604. However, these topical allusions, as many editors note, are too vague to place in any year. The presence of the song in both *Measure for Measure* and the later play, *Rollo, Duke of Normandy* (which adds a second stanza) may only indicate that the King's Men recycled songs whenever possible, as in the case of *Macbeth*, whose Folio text includes cues, but not the verses, for two songs which appear in Middleton's *The Witch*. *Rollo* was, after all, a collaborative play, and the scene in which the song appears was apparently written by John Fletcher; why Middleton and/or Webster would add a song written by Fletcher when they were serving as adapters is difficult to understand. Also, many of the Duke's speeches, beginning with his first in the play's opening lines, seem distanced from the context in which they appear, suggesting that Shakespeare was presenting a man ill at ease in his own environment; if his speeches in Act 3 Scene 1 and Act 4 Scene 1 are seen in the same way, there is no reason to suppose they once belonged in a more fitting spot but were later transposed by an adapter. Lastly, as argued earlier, the nine-months pregnant Juliet is not a 'ghost' character in Act 1 Scene 3 and Act 5 Scene 1 but appears as a visual symbol of the natural consequences of sexual intercourse; as a visual symbol she is abhorrent to the 'precise' Angelo and thus need not speak in each scene in which she appears.

As Brian Gibbons notes, the printed text of *Measure for Measure* 'is mediated to us', and this mediation, through Crane and other King's Men personnel and through compositors, does not remove or distance Shakespeare from the play. His authorial process of making alterations, deviating from his original concepts for characters or plots or themes, working and reworking the text, are apparent and remarkable throughout the text. The final printed text of *Measure for Measure*, reprinted here, represents the collaborative process through which a play-text passed during its transmission from author to theatre to printing house to literary audience. The contributions of Ralph Crane, the King's Men personnel, and the compositors do not darken, distort or peculiarise the play but transmit it as part of the authorial process. This text is not 'ideal' but is 'genuine' enough in re-presenting the way in which Shakespeare's play was ultimately handed down in its printed form.

Select Bibliography

Bald, R.C., ' "Assembled" Texts', *The Library*, 4th ser., vol. 12 (1931–2), pp. 243–8.

Bald, R.C., 'The Foul Papers of a Revision', *The Library*, 4th ser., vol. 26 (1946), pp. 37–50.

Bawcutt, N.W. (ed.), *Measure for Measure* (The Oxford Shakespeare) (Oxford: Oxford University Press, 1991).

Chambers, E.K., *The Disintegration of Shakespeare* (London: Oxford University Press, 1924).

Chambers, E.K., *William Shakespeare: A Study of Facts and Problems*, 2 vols (Oxford: Clarendon Press, 1930).

Cloud, Random (Randall McLeod), 'The Marriage of Good and Bad Quartos', *Shakespeare Quarterly*, vol. 33 (1982), pp. 421–30.

Eccles, Mark (ed.), *A New Variorum Edition of Shakespeare: Measure for Measure* (New York: Modern Language Association, 1980).

Evans, G. Blakemore (text. ed.), *The Riverside Shakespeare* (Boston: Houghton Mifflin, 1974).

Gibbons, Brian (ed.), *Measure for Measure* (The New Cambridge Shakespeare) (Cambridge: Cambridge University Press, 1991).

Greg, W.W., *The Shakespeare First Folio* (Oxford: Clarendon Press, 1955).

Hinman, Charlton, 'Cast-off Copy for the First Folio of Shakespeare', *Shakespeare Quarterly*, vol. 6 (1955), pp. 159–73.

Hinman, Charlton, *The Printing and Proof-Reading of the First Shakespeare Folio*, 2 vols (Oxford: Clarendon Press, 1963).

Hinman, Charlton, *The First Folio of Shakespeare* (New York: W.W. Norton, 1968).

Howard-Hill, T.H., *Ralph Crane and Some Shakespeare First Folio Comedies* (Charlottesville, University Press of Virginia, 1972).

Ioppolo, Grace, *Revising Shakespeare* (Cambridge, Mass.: Harvard University Press, 1991).

Select Bibliography

Johnson, Samuel (ed.), *The Plays of William Shakespeare*, 8 vols (London: J. and R. Tonson, et al., 1765).

Lever, J.W. (ed.), *Measure for Measure* (The Arden Shakespeare) (London: Methuen, 1967).

Malone, Edmond (ed.), *The Plays and Poems of William Shakespeare*, 10 vols (London: H. Baldwin, 1790).

Nosworthy, J.M. (ed.), *Measure for Measure* (The New Penguin Shakespeare) (London: Penguin, 1969).

Pope, Alexander and William Warburton (eds), *The Works of Shakespear*, 8 vols (London: J. and P. Knapton et al., 1747).

Streitberger, W.R., *Collections: Volume XIII: Jacobean and Caroline Revels Accounts 1603–1642* (Oxford: Malone Society, 1986).

Taylor, Gary and John Jowett, *Shakespeare Reshaped: 1606–1623* (Oxford: Clarendon Press, 1993).

Turner, Robert K., 'Revisions and Repetition-Brackets in Fletcher's *A Wife for a Month*', *Studies in Bibliography*, vol. 36 (1983), pp. 178–90.

Wells, Stanley and Gary Taylor (eds), *William Shakespeare: The Complete Works*, and *William Shakespeare: The Complete Works, Original-Spelling Edition* (Oxford: Oxford University Press, 1986).

Wells, Stanley and Gary Taylor, *William Shakespeare: A Textual Companion* (Oxford: Oxford University Press, 1987).

Werstine, Paul, 'Cases and Compositors in the Shakespeare First Folio Comedies', *Studies in Bibliography*, vol. 35 (1982), pp. 206–34.

Wilson, F.P., 'Ralph Crane, Scrivener to the King's Players', *The Library*, 4th ser., vol. 7 (1926), pp. 194–215.

Wilson, J. Dover (ed.), *Measure for Measure* (The Cambridge Shakespeare) (Cambridge: Cambridge University Press, 1922).

Textual History

MEASURE for Measure was first published in the 1623 First Folio under the title 'MEASVRE, / For Measure'. It was entered into the Stationer's Register on 8 November 1623 'for Master Blounte and Isaak Jaggard', along with seven other comedies, two histories and six tragedies, all previously unpublished plays, 'under the hands of Master Doctor WORRALL and Master Cole warden'. The play appears as fourth in the volume (under the heading of 'Comedies'), following *The Tempest*, *The Two Gentlemen of Verona* and *The Merry Wives of Windsor*, all plays, like *Measure for Measure*, printed from Ralph Crane's transcripts. The printed text concludes with a cast-list, probably supplied by Crane, headed '*The Scene Vienna.* / The names of all the Actors'.

The play occupies all of quires F and G in the Folio, and Charlton Hinman noted only two press variants (one of these variants results from uneven inking and may not derive from a press correction in which the printing was stopped and the type corrected or replaced). Hinman identified four compositors, A, B, C and D, but later bibliographers, including T.H. Howard-Hill and Paul Werstine, argue for B, C, D and F. The typesetting of the play was completed in 1622. The text of the play is reprinted in Hinman's facsimile of the First Folio.

Measure for Measure was adapted first by William Davenant in 1662 and next by Charles Gildon, whose version was printed in 1700.

MEASURE,
For Measure.

Actus primus, Scena prima.

Enter Duke, Escalus, Lords.

Duke. Escalus.
Esc. My Lord.
Duk. Of Government, the properties to unfold,
Would seeme in me t'affect speech & discourse,
Since I am put to know, that your owne Science
Exceedes (in that) the lists of all advice
My strength can give you: Then no more remaines
But that, to your sufficiency, as your worth is able,
And let them worke: The nature of our People,
Our *Cities Institutions*, and the Termes
For Common Justice, y'are as pregnant in
As Art, and practise, hath inriched any
That we remember: There is our Commission,
From which, we would not have you warpe; call hither,
I say, bid come before us *Angelo*:
What figure of us thinke you, he will beare.
For you must know, we have with speciall soule
Elected him our absence to supply;

[27]

Measure, For Measure.

Lent him our terror, drest him with our love,
And given his Deputation all the Organs
Of our owne powre: What thinke you of it?
   Esc. If any in *Vienna* be of worth
To undergoe such ample grace, and honour,
It is Lord *Angelo.*

Enter Angelo.

   Duk. Looke where he comes.
   Ang. Alwayes obedient to your Graces will,
I come to know your pleasure.
   Duke. Angelo:
There is a kinde of Character in thy life,
That to th'observer, doth thy history
Fully unfold: Thy selfe, and thy belongings
Are not thine owne so proper, as to waste
Thy selfe upon thy vertues; they on thee:
Heaven doth with us, as we, with Torches doe,
Not light them for themselves: For if our vertues
Did not goe forth of us, 'twere all alike
As if we had them not: Spirits are not finely tonch'd,
But to fine issues: nor nature never lends
The smallest scruple of her excellence,
But like a thrifty goddesse, she determines
Her selfe the glory of a creditour,
Both thanks, and use; but I do bend my speech
To one that can my part in him advertise;
Hold therefore *Angelo:*
In our remove, be thou at full, our selfe:
Mortallitie and Mercie in *Vienna*
Live in thy tongue, and heart: Old *Escalus*
Though first in question, is thy secondary.
Take thy Commission.
   Ang. Now good my Lord
Let there be some more test, made of my mettle,
Before so noble, and so great a figure
Be stamp't upon it.

[28]

Duk. No more evasion:
We have with a leaven'd, and prepared choice
Proceeded to you; therefore take your honors:
Our haste from hence is of so quicke condition,
That it prefers it selfe, and leaves unquestion'd
Matters of needfull value: We shall write to you
As time, and our concernings shall importune,
How it goes with us, and doe looke to know
What doth befall you here. So fare you well:
To th'hopefull execution doe I leave you,
Of your Commissions.

Ang. Yet give leave (my Lord,)
That we may bring you something on the way.

Duk. My haste may not admit it,
Nor neede you (on mine honor) have to doe
With any scruple: your scope is as mine owne,
So to inforce, or qualifie the Lawes
As to your soule seemes good: Give me your hand,
Ile privily away: I love the people,
But doe not like to stage me to their eyes:
Though it doe well, I doe not rellish well
Their lowd applause, and Aves vehement:
Nor doe I thinke the man of safe discretion
That do's affect it. Once more fare you well.

Ang. The heavens give safety to your purposes.

Esc. Lead forth, and bring you backe in happi-
nesse.   *Exit.*

Duk. I thanke you, fare you well.

Esc. I shall desire you, Sir, to give me leave
To have free speech with you; and it concernes me
To looke into the bottome of my place:
A powre I have, but of what strength and nature,
I am not yet instructed.

Ang. 'Tis so with me: Let us with-draw together,
And we may soone our satisfaction have
Touching that point.

Esc. Ile wait upon your honor.   *Exeunt.*

Measure, For Measure.
Scena Secunda.

Enter Lucio, and two other Gentlemen.

Luc. If the *Duke*, with the other Dukes, come not to
composition with the King of *Hungary*, why then all the
Dukes fall upon the King.

1.Gent. Heaven grant us its peace, but not the King
of *Hungaries*.

2.Gent. Amen.

Luc. Thou conclud'st like the Sanctimonious Pirat,
that went to sea with the ten Commandements, but
scrap'd one out of the Table.

2.Gent. Thou shalt not Steale?

Luc. I, that he raz'd.

1.Gent. Why? 'twas a commandement, to command
the Captaine and all the rest from their functions: they
put forth to steale: There's not a Souldier of us all, that
in the thanks-giving before meate, do rallish the petition
well, that praies for peace.

2.Gent. I never heard any Souldier dislike it.

Luc. I beleeve thee: for I thinke thou never was't
where Grace was said.

2.Gent. No? a dozen times at least.

1.Gent. What? In meeter?

Luc. In any proportion. or in any language.

1.Gent. I thinke, or in any Religion.

Luc. I, why not? Grace, is Grace, despight of all con-
troversie: as for example; Thou thy selfe art a wicked
villaine, despight of all Grace.

1.Gent. Well: there went but a paire of sheeres betweene us.

Luc. I grant: as there may betweene the Lists, and
the Velvet. Thou art the List.

1.Gent. And thou the Velvet; thou art good velvet;
thou'rt a three pild-peece I warrant thee: I had as liefe

be a Lyst of an English Kersey, as be pil'd, as thou art
pil'd, for a French Velvet. Do I speake feelingly now?

Luc. I thinke thou do'st: and indeed with most painfull feeling of thy speech: I will, out of thine owne confession, learne to begin thy health; but, whilst I live forget to drinke after thee.

1.Gent. I think I have done my selfe wrong, have I not?

2.Gent. Yes, that thou hast; whether thou art tainted,
or free.   *Enter Bawde.*

Luc. Behold, behold, where Madam *Mitigation* comes.
I have purchas'd as many diseases under her Roofe,
As come to

2.Gent. To what, I pray?

Luc. Judge.

2.Gent. To three thousand Dollours a yeare.

1.Gent. I, and more.

Luc. A French crowne more.

1.Gent. Thou art alwayes figuring diseases in me; but
thou art full of error, I am sound.

Luc. Nay, not (as one would say) healthy: but so
sound, as things that are hollow; thy bones are hollow;
Impiety has made a feast of thee.

1.Gent. How now, which of your hips has the most
profound Ciatica?

Bawd. Well, well: there's one yonder arrested, and
carried to prison, was worth five thousand of you all.

2.Gent. Who's that I pray'thee?

Bawd. Marry Sir, that's *Claudio*, Signior *Claudio*.

1.Gent. *Claudio* to prison? 'tis not so.

Bawd. Nay, but I know 'tis so: I saw him arrested:
saw him carried away: and which is more, within these
three daies his head to be chop'd off.

Luc. But, after all this fooling, I would not have it so:
Art thou sure of this?

Bawd. I am too sure of it: and it is for getting Madam
Julietta with childe.

Luc. Beleeue me this may be: he promis'd to meete

me two howres since, and he was ever precise in promise
keeping.

2.Gent. Besides you know, it drawes somthing neere
to the speech we had to such a purpose.

1.Gent. But most of all agreeing with the proclamation.

Luc. Away: let's goe learne the truth of it.   *Exit.*

Bawd. Thus, what with the war; what with the sweat,
what with the gallowes, and what with poverty, I am
Custom-shrunke. How now? what's the newes with
you.

Enter Clowne.

Clo. Yonder man is carried to prison.

Baw. Well: what has he done?

Clo. A Woman.

Baw. But what's his offence?

Clo. Groping for Trowts, in a peculiar River.

Baw. What? is there a maid with child by him?

Clo. No: but there's a woman with maid by him:
you have not heard of the proclamation, have you?

Baw. What proclamation, man?

Clow. All howses in the Suburbs of *Vienna* must bee
pluck'd downe.

Bawd. And what shall become of those in the Citie?

Clow. They shall stand for seed: they had gon down
to, but that a wise Burger put in for them.

Bawd. But shall our houses of resort in the Suburbs be puld downe?

Clow. To the ground, Mistris.

Bawd. Why heere's a change indeed in the Commonwealth: what shall become of me?

Clow. Come: feare not you: good Counsellors lacke
no Clients: though you change your place, you neede
not change your Trade: Ile bee your Tapster still; courage, there will bee pitty taken on you; you that have
worne your eyes almost out in the service, you will bee
considered.

[32]

Bawd. What's to doe heere, *Thomas* Tapster? let's withdraw?

Clo. Here comes Signior *Claudio*, led by the Provost to prison: and there's Madam *Juliet.*   *Exeunt.*

Scena Tertia.

Enter Provost, Claudio, Juliet, Officers, Lucio, & 2.Gent.

Cla. Fellow, why do'st thou show me thus to th'world?
Beare me to prison, where I am committed.

Pro. I do it not in euill disposition,
But from Lord *Angelo* by speciall charge.

Cla. Thus can the demy-god (Authority)
Make us pay downe, for our offence, by waight
The words of heaven; on whom it will, it will,
On whom it will not (soe) yet still 'tis just.

Luc. Why how now *Claudio*? whence comes this restraint.

Cla. From too much liberty, (my *Lucio*) Liberty
As surfet is the father of much fast,
So every Scope by the immoderate use
Turnes to restraint: Our Natures doe pursue
Like Rats that ravyn downe their proper Bane,
A thirsty euill, and when we drinke, we die.

Luc. If I could speake so wisely under an arrest, I would send for certaine of my Creditors: and yet, to say the truth, I had as lief have the foppery of freedome, as the mortality of imprisonment: what's thy offence, *Claudio*?

Cla. What (but to speake of) would offend againe.

Luc. What, is't murder?

Cla. No.

Luc. Lecherie?

Cla. Call it so.

Pro. Away, Sir, you must goe.

Cla. One word, good friend:
Lucio, a word with you.

[33]

Luc. A hundred:
If they'll doe you any good: Is *Lechery* so look'd after?

Cla. Thus stands it with me: upon a true contract
I got possession of *Julietas* bed,
You know the Lady, she is fast my wife,
Save that we doe the denunciation lacke
Of outward Order. This we came not to,
Onely for propogation of a Dowre
Remaining in the Coffer of her friends,
From whom we thought it meet to hide our Love
Till Time had made them for us. But it chances
The stealth of our most mutuall entertainment
With Character too grosse, is writ on *Juliet.*

Luc. With childe, perhaps?

Cla. Unhappely, even so.
And the new Deputie, now for the Duke,
Whether it be the fault and glimpse of newnes,
Or whether that the body publique, be
A horse whereon the Governor doth ride,
Who newly in the Seate, that it may know
He can command; lets it strait feele the spur:
Whether the Tirranny be in his place,
Or in his Eminence that fills it up
I stagger in: But this new Governor
Awakes me all the inrolled penalties
Which have (like un-scowr'd Armor) hung by th'wall
So long, that ninteene Zodiacks have gone round,
And none of them beene worne; and for a name
Now puts the drowsie and neglected Act
Freshly on me: 'tis surely for a name.

Luc. I warrant it is: And thy head stands so tickle on
thy shoulders, that a milke-maid, if she be in love, may
sigh it off: Send after the Duke, and appeale to him.

Cla. I have done so, but hee's not to be found.
I pre'thee (*Lucio*) doe me this kinde service:
This day, my sister should the Cloyster enter,
And there receive her approbation.

[34]

Acquaint her with the danger of my state,
Implore her, in my voice, that she make friends
To the strict deputie: bid her selfe assay him,
I have great hope in that: for in her youth
There is a prone and speechlesse dialect,
Such as move men: beside, she hath prosperous Art
When she will play with reason, and discourse,
And well she can perswade.

   Luc. I pray shee may; as well for the encouragement
of the like, which else would stand under greevous im-
position: as for the enjoying of thy life, who I would be
sorry should bee thus foolishly lost, at a game of ticke-
tacke: Ile to her.

   Cla. I thanke you good friend *Lucio.*

   Luc. Within two houres.

   Cla. Come Officer, away.   *Exeunt.*

Scena Quarta.

Enter Duke and Frier Thomas.

   Duk. No: holy Father, throw away that thought,
Beleeve not that the dribling dart of Love
Can pierce a compleat bosome: why, I desire thee
To give me secret harbour, hath a purpose
More grave, and wrinkled, then the aims, and ends
Of burning youth.

   Fri. May your Grace speake of it?

   Duk. My holy Sir, none better knowes then you
How I have ever lov'd the life removed
And held in idle price, to haunt assemblies
Where youth, and cost, witlesse bravery keepes.
I have delivered to Lord *Angelo*
(A man of stricture and firme abstinence)
My absolute power, and place here in *Vienna*,
And he supposes me travaild to *Poland*,

(For so I have strewd it in the common eare)
And so it is receiv'd: Now (pious Sir)
You will demand of me, why I do this.

    Fri. Gladly, my Lord.

    Duk. We have strict Statutes, and most biting Laws,
(The needfull bits and curbes to headstrong weedes,)
Which for this foureteene yeares, we have let slip,
Even like an ore-growne Lyon in a Cave
That goes not out to prey: Now, as fond Fathers,
Having bound up the threatning twigs of birch,
Onely to sticke it in their childrens sight,
For terror, not to use: in time the rod
More mock'd, then fear'd: so our Decrees,
Dead to infliction, to themselves are dead,
And libertie, plucks Justice by the nose;
The Baby beates the Nurse, and quite athwart
Goes all decorum.

    Fri. It rested in your Grace
To unloose this tyde-up Justice, when you pleas'd:
And it in you more dreadfull would have seem'd
Then in Lord *Angelo*.

    Duk. I doe feare: too dreadfull:
Sith 'twas my fault, to give the people scope,
'T would be my tirrany to strike and gall them,
For what I bid them doe: For, we bid this be done
When evill deedes have their permissive passe,
And not the punishment: therefore indeede (my father)
I have on *Angelo* impos'd the office,
Who may in th'ambush of my name, strike home,
And yet, my nature never in the fight
To do in slander: And to behold his sway
I will, as 'twere a brother of your Order,
Visit both Prince, and People: Therefore I pre'thee
Supply me with the habit, and instruct me
How I may formally in person beare
Like a true *Frier*: Moe reasons for this action
At our more leysure, shall I render you;

Measure, For Measure.

Onely, this one: Lord *Angelo* is precise,
Stands at a guard with Envie: scarce confesses
That his blood flowes: or that his appetite
Is more to bread then stone; hence shall we see
If power change purpose: what our Seemers be. *Exit.*

Scena Quinta.

Enter Isabell and Francisca a Nun.

Isa. And have you *Nuns* no farther priviledges?
Nun. Are not these large enough?
Isa. Yes truely; I speake not as desiring more,
But rather wishing a more strict restraint
Upon the Sisterstood, the Votarists of Saint *Clare.*

Lucio within.

Luc. Hoa? peace be in this place.
Isa. Who's that which cals?
Nun. It is a mans voice: gentle *Isabella*
Turne you the key, and know his businesse of him;
You may; I may not: you are yet unsworne:
When you have vowd, you must not speake with men,
But in the presence of the *Prioresse*;
Then if you speake, you must not show your face;
Or if you show your face, you must not speake:
He cals againe: I pray you answere him.
Isa. Peace and prosperitie: who is't that cals?
Luc. Haile Virgin, (if you be) as those cheeke-Roses
Proclaime you are no lesse: can you so steed me,
As bring me to the sight of *Isabella*,
A Novice of this place, and the faire Sister
To her unhappie brother *Claudio*?
Isa. Why her unhappy Brother? Let me aske,
The rather for I now must make you know
I am that *Isabella*, and his Sister.

[37]

Measure, For Measure.

Luc. Gentle & faire: your Brother kindly greets you;
Not to be weary with you; he's in prison.

Isa. Woe me; for what?

Luc. For that, which if my selfe might be his Judge,
He should receive his punishment, in thankes:
He hath got his friend with childe.

Isa. Sir, make me not your storie.

Luc. 'Tis true; I would not, though 'tis my familar sin,
With Maids to seeme the Lapwing, and to jest
Tongue, far from heart: play with all Virgins so:
I hold you as a thing en-skied, and sainted,
By your renouncement, an imortall spirit
And to be talk'd with in sincerity,
As with a Saint.

Isa. You doe blaspheme the good, in mocking me.

Luc. Doe not beleeue it: fewnes, and truth; tis thus,
Your brother, and his lover have embrac'd;
As those that feed, grow full, as blossoming Time
That from the seednes, the bare fallow brings
To teemiug foyson: even so her plenteous wombe
Expresseth his full Tilth, and husbandry.

Isa. Some one with childe by him? my cosen *Juliet*?

Luc. Is she your cosen?

Isa. Adoptedly, as schoole-maids change their names
By vaine, though apt affection.

Luc. She it is.

Isa. Oh, let him marry her.

Luc. This is the point.
The Duke is very strangely gone from hence;
Bore many gentlemen (my selfe being one)
In hand, and hope of action: but we doe learne,
By those that know the very Nerves of State,
His giving-out, were of an infinite distance
From his true meant designe: upon his place,
(And with full line of his authority)
Governes Lord *Angelo*; A man, whose blood
Is very snow-broth: one, who never feeles

Measure, For Measure.

The wanton stings, and motions of the sence;
But doth rebate, and blunt his naturall edge
With profits of the minde; Studie, and fast
He (to give feare to use, and libertie,
Which have, for long, run-by the hideous law,
As Myce, by Lyons) hath pickt out an act,
Under whose heavy sence, your brothers life
Fals into forfeit: he arrests him on it,
And followes close the rigor of the Statute
To make him an example: all hope is gone,
Unlesse you have the grace, by your faire praier
To soften *Angelo*: And that's my pith of businesse
'Twixt you, and your poore brother.

    Isa. Doth he so,
Seeke his life?

    Luc. Has censur'd him already,
And as I heare, the Provost hath a warrant
For's execution.

    Isa. Alas what poore
Abilitie's in me, to doe him good.

    Luc. Assay the powre you have.

    Isa. My power? alas, I doubt.

    Luc. Our doubts are traitors
And makes us loose the good we oft might win,
By fearing to attempt: Goe to Lord *Angelo*
And let him learne to know, when Maidens sue
Men give like gods: but when they weepe and kneele,
All their petitions, are as freely theirs
As they themselves would owe them.

    Isa. Ile see what I can doe.

    Luc. But speedily.

    Isa. I will about it strait;
No longer staying, but to give the Mother
Notice of my affaire: I humbly thanke you:
Commend me to my brother: soone at night
Ile send him certaine word of my successe.

    Luc. I take my leave of you.

Isa. Good sir, adieu.   *Exeunt.*

Actus Secundus. Scoena Prima.

Enter Angelo, Escalus, and servants, Justice.

Ang. We must not make a scar-crow of the Law,
Setting it up to feare the Birds of prey,
And let it keepe one shape, till custome make it
Their pearch, and not their terror.
   Esc. I, but yet
Let us be keene, and rather cut a little
Then fall, and bruise to death: alas, this gentleman
Whom I would save, had a most noble father,
Let but your honour know
(Whom I beleeve to be most strait in vertue)
That in the working of your owne affections,
Had time coheard with Place, or place with wishing,
Or that the resolute acting of our blood
Could have attaind th'effect of your owne purpose,
Whether you had not sometime in your life
Er'd in this point, which now you censure him,
And puld the Law upon you.
   Ang. 'Tis one thing to be tempted (*Escalus*)
Another thing to fall: I not deny
The Jury passing on the Prisoners life
May in the sworne-twelve have a thiefe, or two
Guiltier then him they try; what's open made to Justice,
That Justice ceizes; What knowes the Lawes
That theeves do passe on theeves? 'Tis very pregnant,
The Jewell that we finde, we stoope, and take't,
Because we see it; but what we doe not see,
We tread upon, and never thinke of it.
You may not so extenuate his offence,
For I have had such faults; but rather tell me
When I, that censure him, do so offend,

Let mine owne Judgement patterne out my death,
And nothing come in partiall. Sir, he must dye.

Enter Provost.

Esc. Be it as your wisedome will.
Ang. Where is the *Provost*?
Pro. Here if it like your honour.
Ang. See that *Claudio*
Be executed by nine to morrow morning,
Bring him his Confessor, let him be prepar'd,
For that's the utmost of his pilgrimage.
Esc. Well: heaven forgive him; and forgive us all:
Some rise by sinne, and some by vertue fall:
Some run from brakes of Ice, and answere none,
And some condemned for a fault alone.

Enter Elbow, Froth, Clowne, Officers.

Elb. Come, bring them away: if these be good people in a Common weale, that doe nothing but use their
abuses in common houses, I know no law: bring them
away.
Ang. How now Sir, what's your name? And what's
the matter?
Elb. If it please your honour, I am the poore Dukes
Constable, and my name is *Elbow*; I doe leane upon Ju-
stice Sir, and doe bring in here before your good honor,
two notorious Benefactors.
Ang. Benefactors? Well: What Benefactors are they?
Are they not Malefactors?
Elb. It if please your honour, I know not well what
they are: But precise villaines they are, that I am sure of
and void of all prophanation in the world, that good
Christians ought to have.
Esc. This comes off well: here's a wise Officer.
Ang. Goe to: what quality are they of? *Elbow* is
your name?
Why do'st thou not speake *Elbow*?

[41]

Clo. He cannot Sir: he's out at Elbow.

Ang. What are you Sir?

Elb. He Sir: a Tapster Sir: parcell Baud: one that serves a bad woman: whose house Sir was (as they say) pluckt downe in the Suborbs: and now she professes a hot-house; which, I thinke is a very ill house too.

Esc. How know you that?

Elb. My wife Sir? whom I detest before heaven, and your honour.

Esc. How? thy wife?

Elb. I Sir: whom I thanke heaven is an honest woman.

Esc. Do'st thou detest her therefore?

Elb. I say sir, I will detest my selfe also, as well as she, that this house, if it be not a Bauds house, it is pitty of her life, for it is a naughty house.

Esc. How do'st thou know that, Constable?

Elb. Marry sir, by my wife, who if she had bin a woman Cardinally given, might have bin accus'd in fornication, adultery, and all uncleanlinesse there.

Esc. By the womans meanes?

Elb. I sir, by Mistris *Over-dons* meanes: but as she spit in his face, so she defide him.

Clo. Sir, if it please your honor, this is not so.

Elb. Prove it before these varlets here, thou honorable man, prove it.

Esc. Doe you heare how he misplaces?

Clo. Sir, she came in great with childe: and longing (saving your honors reverence) for stewd prewyns; sir, we had but two in the house, which at that very distant time stood, as it were in a fruit dish (a dish of some three pence; your honours have seene such dishes) they are not China-dishes, but very good dishes.

Esc. Go too: go too: no matter for the dish sir.

Clo. No indeede sir not of a pin; you are therein in the right: but, to the point: As I say, this Mistris *Elbow*, being (as I say) with childe, and being great bellied, and

Measure, For Measure.

longing (as I said) for prewyns: and having but two in
the dish (as I said) Master *Froth* here, this very man, having eaten the rest (as I said) & (as I say) paying for them
very honestly: for, as you know Master *Froth*, I could not
give you three pence againe.

Fro. No indeede.

Clo. Very well: you being then (if you be remembred) cracking the stones of the foresaid prewyns.

Fro. I, so I did indeede.

Clo. Why, very well: I telling you then (if you be
remembred) that such a one, and such a one, were past
cure of the thing you wot of, unlesse they kept very good
diet, as I told you.

Fro. All this is true.

Clo. Why very well then.

Esc. Come: you are a tedious foole: to the purpose:
what was done to *Elbowes* wife, that hee hath cause to
complaine of? Come me to what was done to her.

Clo. Sir, your honor cannot come to that yet.

Esc. No sir, nor I meane it not.

Clo. Sir, but you shall come to it, by your honours
leave: And I beseech you, looke into Master *Froth* here
sir, a man of four-score pound a yeare; whose father
died at *Hallowmas*: Was't not at *Hallowmas* Master
Froth?

Fro. Allhallond-Eve.

Clo. Why very well: I hope here be truthes: he Sir,
sitting (as I say) in a lower chaire, Sir, 'twas in the bunch
of Grapes, where indeede you have a delight to sit, have
you not?

Fro. I have so, because it is an open roome, and good
for winter.

Clo. Why very well then: I hope here be truthes.

Ang. This will last out a night in *Russia*
When nights are longest there: Ile take my leave,
And leave you to the hearing of the cause;
Hoping youle finde good cause to whip them all.   *Exit.*

[43]

Esc. I thinke no lesse: good morrow to your Lordship. Now Sir, come on: What was done to *Elbowes*
wife, once more?

Clo. Once Sir? there was nothing done to her once.

Elb. I beseech you Sir, aske him what this man did to
my wife.

Clo. I beseech your honor, aske me.

Esc. Well sir, what did this Gentleman to her?

Clo. I beseech you sir, looke in this Gentlemans face:
good Master *Froth* looke upon his honor; 'tis for a good
purpose: doth your honor marke his face?

Esc. I sir, very well.

Clo. Nay, I beseech you marke it well.

Esc. Well, I doe so.

Clo. Doth your honor see any harme in his face?

Esc. Why no.

Clo. Ile be supposd upon a booke, his face is the worst
thing about him: good then: if his face be the worst
thing about him, how could Master *Froth* doe the Con-
stables wife any harme? I would know that of your
honour.

Esc. He's in the right (Constable) what say you to it?

Elb. First, and it like you, the house is a respected
house; next, this is a respected fellow; and his Mistris is
a respected woman.

Clo. By this hand Sir, his wife is a more respected person then any of us all.

Elb. Varlet, thou lyest: thou lyest wicked varlet: the
time is yet to come that shee was ever respected with
man, woman, or childe.

Clo. Sir, she was respected with him, before he married with her.

Esc. Which is the wiser here; *Justice* or *Iniquitie*? Is
this true?

Elb. O thou caytiffe: O thou varlet: O thou wicked *Hanniball*; I respected with her, before I was married
to her? If ever I was respected with her, or she with me,

[44]

let not your worship thinke mee the poore *Dukes* Officer: prove this, thou wicked *Hanniball*, or ile have
mine action of battry on thee.

Esc. If he tooke you a box 'oth'eare, you might have
your action of slander too.

Elb. Marry I thanke your good worship for it: what
is't your Worships pleasure I shall doe with this wicked Caitiffe?

Esc. Truly Officer, because he hath some offences in
him, that thou wouldst discover, if thou couldst, let him
continue in his courses, till thou knowst what they are.

Elb. Marry I thanke your worship for it: Thou seest
thou wicked varlet now, what's come upon thee. Thou
art to continue now thou Varlet, thou art to continue.

Esc. Where were you borne, friend?

Fro. Here in *Vienna*, Sir.

Esc. Are you of fourescore pounds a yeere?

Fro. Yes, and 't please you sir.

Esc. So: what trade are you of, sir?

Clo. A Tapster, a poore widdowes Tapster.

Esc. Your Mistris name?

Clo. Mistris *Over-don*.

Esc. Hath she had any more than one husband?

Clo. Nine, sir: *Over-don* by the last.

Esc. Nine? come hether to me, Master *Froth*; Master
Froth, I would not have you acquainted with Tapsters;
they will draw you Master *Froth*, and you wil hang them:
get you gon, and let me heare no more of you.

Fro. I thanke your worship: for mine owne part, I
never come into any roome in a Tap-house, but I am
drawne in.

Esc. Well: no more of it Master *Froth*: farewell:
Come you hether to me, M^r. Tapster: what's your name
M^r. Tapster?

Clo. *Pompey*.

Esc. What else?

Clo. *Bum*, Sir.

Esc. Troth, and your bum is the greatest thing about you, so that in the beastliest sence, you are *Pompey* the great; *Pompey*, you are partly a bawd, *Pompey*; howsoever you colour it in being a Tapster, are you not? come, tell me true, it shall be the better for you.

Clo. Truly sir, I am a poore fellow that would live.

Esc. How would you live *Pompey*? by being a bawd? what doe you thinke of the trade *Pompey*? is it a lawfull trade?

Clo. If the Law would allow it, sir.

Esc. But the Law will not allow it *Pompey*; nor it shall not be allowed in *Vienna*.

Clo. Do's your Worship meane to geld and splay all the youth of the City?

Esc. No, *Pompey*.

Clo. Truely Sir, in my poore opinion they will too't then: if your worship will take order for the drabs and the knaves, you need not to feare the bawds.

Esc. There is pretty orders beginning I can tell you: It is but heading, and hanging.

Clo. If you head, and hang all that offend that way but for ten yeare together; you'll be glad to give out a Commission for more heads: if this law hold in *Vienna* ten yeare, ile rent the fairest house in it after three pence a Bay: if you live to see this come to passe, say *Pompey* told you so.

Esc. Thanke you good *Pompey*; and in requitall of your prophesie, harke you: I advise you let me not finde you before me againe upon any complaint whatsoever; no, not for dwelling where you doe: if I doe *Pompey*, I shall beat you to your Tent, and prove a shrewd *Cesar* to you: in plaine dealing *Pompey*, I shall have you whipt; so for this time, *Pompey*, fare you well.

Clo. I thanke your Worship for your good counsell; but I shall follow it as the flesh and fortune shall better determine. Whip me? no, no let Carman whip his Jade, The valiant heart's not whipt out of his trade.   *Exit.*

Esc. Come hether to me, Master *Elbow*: come hither
Master Constable: how long have you bin in this place
of Constable?

Elb. Seven yeere, and a halfe sir.

Esc. I thought by the readinesse in the office, you had
continued in it some time: you say seaven yeares together.

Elb. And a halfe sir.

Esc. Alas, it hath beene great paines to you: they do
you wrong to put you so oft upon't. Are there not men
in your Ward sufficient to serve it?

Elb. 'Faith sir, few of any wit in such matters: as they
are chosen, they are glad to choose me for them; I do it
for some peece of money, and goe through with all.

Esc. Looke you bring mee in the names of some sixe
or seven, the most sufficient of your parish.

Elb. To your Worships house sir?

Esc. To my house: fare you well: what's a clocke,
thinke you?

Just. Eleven, Sir.

Esc. I pray you home to dinner with me.

Just. I humbly thanke you.

Esc. It grieves me for the death of *Claudio*
But there's no remedie:

Just. Lord *Angelo* is severe.

Esc. It is but needfull.
Mercy is not it selfe, that oft lookes so,
Pardon is still the nurse of second woe:
But yet, poore *Claudio*, there is no remedie.
Come Sir.   *Exeunt.*

Scena Secunda.

Enter Provost, Servant.

Ser. Hee's hearing of a Cause; he will come straight,

I'le tell him of you.

Pro. 'Pray you doe; Ile know
His pleasure, may be he will relent; alas
He hath but as offended in a dreame,
All Sects, all Ages smack of this vice, and he
To die for't?

Enter Angelo.

Ang. Now, what's the matter *Provost*?
Pro. Is it your will *Claudio* shall die tomorrow?
Ang. Did not I tell thee yea? hast thou not order?
Why do'st thou aske againe?
Pro. Lest I might be too rash:
Under your good correction, I have seene
When after execution, Judgement hath
Repented ore his doome.
Ang. Goe to; let that be mine,
Doe you your office, or give up your Place,
And you shall well be spar'd.
Pro. I crave your Honours pardon:
What shall be done Sir, with the groaning *Juliet*?
Shee's very neere her howre.
Ang. Dispose of her
To some more fitter place; and that with speed.
Ser. Here is the sister of the man condemn'd,
Desires accesse to you.
Ang. Hath he a Sister?
Pro. I my good Lord, a very vertuous maid,
And to be shortlie of a Sister-hood,
If not alreadie.
Ang. Well: let her be admitted,
See you the Fornicatress be remov'd,
Let her have needfull, but not lavish meanes,
There shall be order for't.

Enter Lucio and Isabella.

Pro. 'Save your Honour.

Measure, For Measure.

Ang. Stay a little while: y'are welcome: what's your will?

Isab. I am a wofull Sutor to your Honour,
'Please but your Honor heare me.

Ang. Well: what's your suite.

Isab. There is a vice that most I doe abhorre,
And most desire should meet the blow of Justice;
For which I would not plead, but that I must,
For which I must not plead, but that I am
At warre, twixt will, and will not.

Ang. Well: the matter?

Isab. I have a brother is condemn'd to die,
I doe beseech you let it be his fault,
And not my brother.

Pro. Heaven give thee moving graces.

Ang. Condemne the fault, and not the actor of it,
Why every fault's condemnd ere it be done:
Mine were the verie Cipher of a Function
To fine the faults, whose fine stands in record,
And let goe by the Actor.

Isab. O just, but severe Law:
I had a brother then; heaven keepe your honour.

Luc. Give't not ore so: to him againe, entreat him,
Kneele downe before him, hang upon his gowne,
You are too cold: if you should need a pin,
You could not with more tame a tongue desire it:
To him, I say.

Isab. Must he needs die?

Ang. Maiden, no remedie.

Isab. Yes: I doe thinke that you might pardon him,
And neither heaven, nor man grieve at the mercy.

Ang. I will not doe't.

Isab. But can you if you would?

Ang. Looke what I will not, that I cannot doe.

Isab. But might you doe't & do the world no wrong
If so your heart were touch'd with that remorse,
As mine is to him?

Ang. Hee's senteenc'd, tis too late.

[49]

Luc. You are too cold.

Isab. Too late? why no: I that doe speak a word
May call it againe: well, beleeve this
No ceremony that to great ones longs,
Not the Kings Crowne; nor the deputed sword,
The Marshalls Truncheon, nor the Judges Robe
Become them with one halfe so good a grace
As mercie does: If he had bin as you, and you as he,
You would have slipt like him, but he like you
Would not have been so sterne.

Ang. Pray you be gone.

Isab. I would to heaven I had your potencie,
And you were *Isabell*: should it then be thus?
No: I would tell what 'twere to be a Judge,
And what a prisoner.

Luc. I, touch him: there's the vaine.

Ang. Your Brother is a forfeit of the Law,
And you but waste your words.

Isab. Alas, alas:
Why all the soules that were, were forfeit once,
And he that might the vantage best have tooke,
Found out the remedie: how would you be,
If he, which is the top of Judgement, should
But judge you, as you are? Oh, thinke on that,
And mercie then will breathe within your lips
Like man new made.

Ang. Be you content, (faire Maid)
It is the Law, not I, condemne your brother,
Were he my kinsman, brother, or my sonne,
It should be thus with him: he must die tomorrow.

Isab. To morrow? oh, that's sodaine,
Spare him, spare him:
Hee's not prepar'd for death; even for our kitchins
We kill the fowle of season: shall we serve heaven
With lesse respect then we doe minister
To our grosse-selves? good, good my Lord, bethink you;

Who is it that hath di'd for this offence?
There's many have committed it.

   Luc. I, well said.

   Ang. The Law hath not bin dead, though it hath slept
Those many had not dar'd to doe that evill
If the first, that did th' Edict infringe
Had answer'd for his deed. Now 'tis awake,
Takes note of what is done, and like a Prophet
Lookes in a glasse that shewes what future evils
Either now, or by remissenesse, new conceiv'd,
And so in progresse to be hatc'hd, and borne,
Are now to have no successive degrees,
But here they live to end.

   Isab. Yet shew some pittie.

   Ang. I shew it most of all, when I show Justice;
For then I pittie those I doe not know,
Which a dismis'd offence, would after gaule
And doe him right, that answering one foule wrong
Lives not to act another. Be satisfied;
Your Brother dies to morrow; be content.

   Isab. So you must be ye first that gives this sentence,
And hee, that suffers: Oh it is excellent
To have a Giants strength: but it is tyrannous
To use it like a Giant.

   Luc. That's well said.

   Isab. Could great men thunder
As *Jove* himselfe do's, *Jove* would never be quiet,
For every pelting petty Officer
Would use his heaven for thunder;
Nothing but thunder: Mercifull heaven,
Thou rather with thy sharpe and sulpherous bolt
Splits the un-wedgable and gnarled Oke,
Then the soft Mertill: But man, proud man,
Drest in a little briefe authoritie,
Most ignorant of what he's most assur'd,
(His glassie Essence) like an angry Ape

[51]

Plaies such phantastique tricks before high heaven,
As makes the Angels weepe: who with our spleenes,
Would all themselves laugh mortall.

Luc. Oh, to him, to him wench: he will relent,
Hee's comming: I perceive't.

Pro. Pray heaven she win him.

Isab. We cannot weigh our brother with our selfe,
Great men may jest with Saints: tis wit in them,
But in the lesse fowle prophanation.

Luc. Thou'rt i'th right (Girle) more o'that.

Isab. That in the Captaine's but a chollericke word,
Which in the Souldier is flat blasphemie.

Luc. Art avis'd o'that? more on't.

Ang. Why doe you put these sayings upon me?

Isab. Because Authoritie, though it erre like others,
Hath yet a kinde of medicine in it selfe
That skins the vice o'th top; goe to your bosome,
Knock there, and aske your heart what it doth know
That's like my brothers fault: if it confesse
A naturall guiltinesse, such as is his,
Let it not sound a thought upon your tongue
Against my brothers life.

Ang. Shee speakes, and 'tis such sence
That my Sence breeds with it; fare you well.

Isab. Gentle my Lord, turne backe.

Ang. I will bethinke me: come againe to morrow.

Isa. Hark, how Ile bribe you: good my Lord turn back.

Ang. How? bribe me?

Is. I, with such gifts that heaven shall share with you.

Luc. You had mar'd all else.

Isab. Not with fond Sickles of the tested-gold,
Or Stones, whose rate are either rich, or poore
As fancie values them: but with true prayers,
That shall be up at heaven, and enter there
Ere Sunne rise: prayers from preserved soules,
From fasting Maides, whose mindes are dedicate
To nothing temporall.

Ang. Well: come to me to morrow.

Luc. Goe to: 'tis well; away.

Isab. Heaven keepe your honour safe

Ang. Amen.

For I am that way going to temptation,

Where prayers crosse.

Isab. At what hower to morrow,

Shall I attend your Lordship?

Ang. At any time 'fore-noone.

Isab. 'Save your Honour.

Ang. From thee: even from thy vertue.

What's this? what's this? is this her fault, or mine?

The Tempter, or the Tempted, who sins most? ha?

Not she: nor doth she tempt: but it is I,

That, lying by the Violet in the Sunne,

Doe as the Carrion do's, not as the flowre,

Corrupt with vertuous season: Can it be,

That Modesty may more betray our Sence

Then womans lightnesse? having waste ground enough,

Shall we desire to raze the Sanctuary

And pitch our evils there? oh fie, fie, fie: ·

What dost thou? or what art thou *Angelo*?

Dost thou desire her fowly, for those things

That make her good? oh, let her brother live:

Theeves for their robbery have authority,

When Judges steale themselves: what, doe I love her,

That I desire to heare her speake again?

And feast upon her eyes? what is't I dreame on?

Oh cunning enemy, that to catch a Saint,

With Saints dost bait thy hooke: most dangerous

Is that temptation, that doth goad us on

To sinne, in loving vertue: never could the Strumpet

With all her double vigor, Art, and Nature

Once stir my temper: but this vertuous Maid

Subdues me quite: Ever till now

When men were fond, I smild, and wondred how. *Exit.*

Measure, For Measure.
Scena Tertia.

Enter Duke and Provost.

Duke. Haile to you, *Provost*, so I thinke you are.
Pro. I am the Provost: whats your will, good Frier?
Duke. Bound by my charity, and my blest order,
I come to visite the afflicted spirits
Here in the prison: doe me the common right
To let me see them: and to make me know
The nature of their crimes, that I may minister
To them accordingly.
Pro. I would do more then that, if more were needfull

Enter Juliet.

Looke here comes one: a Gentlewoman of mine,
Who falling in the flawes of her owne youth,
Hath blisterd her report: She is with childe,
And he that got it sentenc'd: a yong man,
More fit to doe another such offence,
Then dye for this.
Duk. When must he dye?
Pro. As I do thinke to morrow.
I have provided for you, stay a while
And you shall be conducted.
Duk. Repent you (faire one) of the sin you carry?
Jul. I doe; and beare the shame most patiently.
Du. Ile teach you how you shal araign your conscience
And try your penitence, if it be sound,
Or hollowly put on.
Jul. Ile gladly learne.
Duk. Love you the man that wrong'd you?
Jul. Yes, as I love the woman that wrong'd him.
Duk. So then it seemes your most offence full act
Was mutually committed.
Jul. Mutually.

[54]

Duk. Then was your sin of heavier kinde then his.

Jul. I doe confess it, and repent it (Father.)

Duk. 'Tis meet so (daughter) but least you do repent
As that the sin hath brought you to this shame,
Which sorrow is alwaies toward our selves, not heaven,
Showing we would not spare heaven, as we love it,
But as we stand in feare.

Jul. I doe repent me, as it is an evill,
And take the shame with joy.

Duk. There rest:
Your partner (as I heare) must die to morrow,
And I am going with instruction to him:
Grace goe with you, *Benedicite.*   *Exit.*

Jul. Must die to morrow? oh injurious Love
That respits me a life, whose very comfort
Is still a dying horror.

Pro. 'Tis pitty of him.   *Exeunt.*

Scena Quarta.

Enter Angelo.

Ang. When I would pray, & think, I thinke, and pray
To severall subjects: heaven hath my empty words,
Whilst my Invention, hearing not my Tongue,
Anchors on *Isabell*: heaven in my mouth,
As if I did but onely chew his name,
And in my heart the strong and swelling evill
Of my conception: the state whereon I studied
Is like a good thing, being often read
Growne feard, and tedious: yea, my Gravitie
Wherein (let no man heare me) I take pride,
Could I, with boote, change for an idle plume
Which the ayre beats for vaine: oh place, oh forme,
How often dost thou with thy case, thy habit
Wrench awe from fooles, and tye the wiser soules
To thy false seeming? Blood, thou art blood,

Let's write good Angell on the Devills horne
'Tis not the Devills Crest: how now? who's there?

Enter Servant.

Ser. One *Isabell*, a Sister, desires accesse to you.
Ang. Teach her the way: oh, heavens
Why doe's my bloud thus muster to my heart,
Making both it unable for it selfe,
And dispossessing all my other parts
Of necessary fitnesse?
So play the foolish throngs with one that swounds,
Come all to help him, and so stop the ayre
By which hee should revive: and even so
The generall subject to a wel-wisht King
Quit their owne part, and in obsequious fondnesse
Crowd to his presence, where their un-taught love
Must needs appear offence: how now faire Maid.

Enter Isabella.

Isab. I am come to know your pleasure.
An. That you might know it, wold much better please me,
Then to demand what 'tis: your Brother cannot live.
Isab. Even so: heaven keepe your Honor.
Ang. Yet may he live a while: and it may be
As long as you, or I: yet he must die.
Isab. Under your Sentence?
Ang. Yea.
Isab. When, I beseech you: that in his Reprieve
(Longer, or shorter) he may be so fitted
That his soule sicken not.
Ang. Ha? fie, these filthy vices: It were as good
To pardon him, that hath from nature stolne
A man already made, as to remit
Their sawcie sweetnes, that do coyne heavens Image
In stamps that are forbid: 'tis all as easie,
Falsely to take away a life true made,
As to put mettle in restrained meanes
To make a false one.

Isab. 'Tis set downe so in heaven, but not in earth.

Ang. Say you so: then I shall poze you quickly.
Which had you rather, that the most just Law
Now tooke your brothers life, and to redeeme him
Give up your body to such sweet uncleannesse
As she that he hath staind?

Isab. Sir, beleeve this.
I had rather give my body, then my soule.

Ang. I talke not of your soule: our compel'd sins
Stand more for number, then for accompt.

Isab. How say you?

Ang. Nay Ile not warrant that: for I can speake
Against the thing I say: Answere to this,
I (now the voyce of the recorded Law)
Pronounce a sentence on your Brothers life,
Might there not be a charitie in sinne,
To save this Brothers life?

Isab. Please you to doo't,
Ile take it as a perill to my soule,
It is no sinne at all, but charitie.

Ang. Pleas'd you to doo't, at perill of your soule
Were equall poize of sinne, and charitie.

Isab. That I do beg his life, if it be sinne
Heaven let me beare it: you granting of my suit,
It that be sin, Ile make it my Morne-praier,
To have it added to the faults of mine,
And nothing of your answere.

Ang. Nay, but heare me,
Your sence pursues not mine: either you are ignorant,
Or seeme so crafty; and that's not good.

Isab. Let be ignorant, and in nothing good,
But graciously to know I am no better.

Ang. Thus wisdome wishes to appeare most bright,
When it doth taxe it selfe: As these blacke Masques
Proclaime an en-shield beauty ten times louder
Then beauty could displaied: But marke me,
To be received plaine, Ile speake more grosse:

[57]

Your Brother is to dye.

Isab. So.

Ang. And his offence is so, as it appeares,
Accountant to the Law, upon that paine.

Isab. True.

Ang. Admit no other way to save his life
(As I subscribe not that, nor any other,
But in the losse of question) that you, his Sister,
Finding your selfe desir'd of such a person,
Whose creadit with the Judge, or owne great place,
Could fetch your Brother from the Manacles
Of the all-building-Law: and that there were
No earthly meane to save him, but that either
You must lay downe the treasures of your body,
To this supposed, or else to let him suffer:
What would you doe?

Isab. As much for my poore Brother as my selfe;
That is: were I under the tearmes of death,
Th'impression of keene whips, I'ld weare as Rubies,
And strip my selfe to death, as to a bed,
That longing have bin sicke for, ere I'ld yeeld
My body up to shame.

Ang. Then must your brother die.

Isa. And 'twer the cheaper way:
Better it were a brother dide at once,
Then that a sister, by redeeming him
Should die for ever.

Ang. Were not you then as cruell as the Sentence,
That you have slander'd so?

Isa. Ignomie in ransome, and free pardon
Are of two houses: lawfull mercie,
Is nothing kin to fowle redemption.

Ang. You seem'd of late to make the Law a tirant,
And rather prov'd the sliding of your brother
A merriment, then a vice.

Isa. Oh pardon me my Lord, it oft fals out
To have, what we would have,

[58]

We speake not what we meane;
I something do excuse the thing I hate,
For his advantage that I dearely love.
    Ang. We are all fraile.
    Isa. Else let my brother die,
If not a fedarie but onely he
Owe, and succeed thy weakenesse.
    Ang. Nay, women are fraile too.
    Isa. I, as the glasses where they view themselves,
Which are as easie broke as they make formes:
Women? Helpe heaven; men their creation marre
In profiting by them: Nay, call us ten times fraile,
For we are soft, as our complexions are,
And credulous to false prints.
    Ang. I thinke it well:
And from this testimonie of your owne sex
(Since I suppose we are made to be no stronger
Then faults may shake our frames) let me be bold;
I do arrest your words. Be that you are,
That is a woman; if you be more, you'r none.
If you be one (as you are well exprest
By all externall warrants) shew it now,
By putting on the destin'd Liverie.
    Isa. I have no tongue but one; gentle my Lord,
Let me entreate you speake the former language.
    Ang. Plainlie conceive I love you.
    Isa. My brother did love *Juliet*,
And you tell me that he shall die for't.
    Ang. He shall not *Isabell* if you give me love.
    Isa. I know your vertue hath a licence in't,
Which seemes a little fouler then it is,
To plucke on others.
    Ang. Beleeve me on mine Honor,
My words expresse my purpose.
    Isa. Ha? Little honor to be much beleev'd,
And most pernitious purpose: Seeming, seeming.
I will proclaime thee *Angelo*, looke for't.

Signe me a present pardon for my brother,
Or with an out-stretcht throate Ile tell the world aloud
What man thou art.
   Ang. Who will beleeve thee *Isabell*?
My unsoild name, th'austeerenesse of my life,
My vouch against you, and my place i'th State,
Will so your accusation over-weigh,
That you shall stifle in your owne reporr,
And smell of calumnie. I have begun,
And now I give my sensuall race, the reine,
Fit thy consent to my sharpe appetite,
Lay by all nicetie, and prolixious blushes
That banish what thy sue for: Redeeme thy brother,
By yeelding up thy bodie to my will,
Or else he must not onelie die the death,
But thy unkindnesse shall his death draw out
To lingring sufferance: Answer me to morrow,
Or by the affection that now guides me most,
Ile prove a Tirant to him. As for you,
Say what you can; my false, ore-weighs your true.   *Exit*
   Isa. To whom should I complaine? Did I tell this,
Who would beleeve me? O perilous mouthes
That beare in them, one and the selfesame tongue,
Either of condemnation, or approofe,
Bidding the Law make cursie to their will,
Hooking both right and wrong to th'appetite,
To follow as it drawes. Ile to my brother,
Though he hath falne by prompture of the blood,
Yet hath he in him such a minde of Honor,
That had he twentie heads to tender downe
On twentie bloodie blockes, hee'ld yeeld them up,
Before his sister should her bodie stoope
To such abhord pollution.
Then *Isabell* live chaste, and brother die;
"More then our Brother, is our Chastitie.
Ile tell him yet of *Angelo*'s request,
And fit his minde to death, for his soules rest.   *Exit*.

Measure, For Measure.

Actus Tertius. Scena Prima.

Enter Duke, Claudio, and Provost.

Du. So then you hope of pardon from Lord *Angelo*?
Cla. The miserable have no other medicine
But onely hope: I'have hope to live, and am prepar'd to
die.
Duke. Be absolute for death: either death or life
Shall thereby be the sweeter. Reason thus with life:
If I do loose thee, I do loose a thing
That none but fooles woulde keepe: a breath thou art,
Servile to all the skyie-influences,
That dost this habitation where thou keepst
Hourely afflict: Meerely, thou art deaths foole,
For him thou labourst by thy flight to shun,
And yet runst toward him still. Thou art not noble,
For all th'accommodations that thou bearst,
Are nurst by basenesse: Thou'rt by no meanes valiant,
For thou dost feare the soft and tender forke
Of a poore worme: thy best of rest is sleepe,
And that thou oft provoakst, yet grosselie fearst
Thy death, which is no more. Thou art not thy selfe,
For thou exists on manie a thousand graines
That issue out of dust. Happie thou art not,
For what thou hast not, still thou striv'st to get,
And what thou hast forgetst. Thou art not certaine,
For thy complexion shifts to strange effects,
After the Moone: If thou art rich, thou'rt poore,
For like an Asse, whose backe with Ingots bowes;
Thou bearst thy heavie riches but a journie,
And death unloads thee; Friend hast thou none.
For thine owne bowels which do call thee, fire
The meere effusion of thy proper loines
Do curse the Gowt, Sapego, and the Rheume
For ending thee no sooner. Thou has nor youth, nor age
But as it were an after-dinners sleepe

[61]

Measure, For Measure.

Dreaming on both, for all thy blessed youth
Becomes as aged, and doth begge the almes
Of palsied-Eld: and when thou art old, and rich
Thou hast neither heate, affection, limbe, nor beautie
To make thy riches pleasant: what's yet in this
That beares the name of life? Yet in this life
Lie hid moe thousand deaths; yet death we feare
That makes these oddes, all even.
    Cla. I humblie thanke you.
To sue to live, I finde I seeke to die,
And seeking death, finde life: Let it come on.

Enter Isabella.

    Isab. What hoa? Pleace heere; Grace, and good com-
panie.
    Pro. Who's there? Come in, the wish deserves a
welcome.
    Duke. Deere sir, ere long Ile visit you againe.
    Cla. Most holie Sir, I thanke you.
    Isa. My businesse is a word or two with *Claudio.*
    Pro. And verie welcom: looke Signior, here's your
sister.
    Duke. Provost, a word with you.
    Pro. As manie as you please.
    Duke. Bring them to heare me speak, where I may be
conceal'd.
    Cla. Now sister, what's the comfort?
    Isa. Why,
As all comforts are: most good, most good indeede,
Lord *Angelo* having affaires to heaven
Intends you for his swift Ambassador,
Where you shall be an everlasting Leiger;
Therefore your best appointment make with speed,
To Morrow you set on.
    Clau. Is there no remedie?
    Isa. None, but such remedie, as to save a head
To cleave a heart in twaine:

Measure, For Measure.

Clau. But is there anie?

Isa. Yes brother, you may live;
There is a divellish mercie in the Judge,
If you'l implore it, that will free your life,
But fetter you till death.

Cla. Perpetuall durance?

Isa. I just, perpetuall durance, a restraint
Through all the worlds vastiditie you had
To a determin'd scope.

Cla. But in what nature?

Isa. In such a one, as you consenting too't,
Would barke your honor from that trunke you beare,
And leave you naked.

Cla. Let me know the point.

Isa. Oh, I do feare thee *Claudio*, and I quake,
Least thou a feavorous life shouldst entertaine,
And six or seven winters more respect
Then a perpetuall Honor. Dar'st thou die?
The sence of death is most in apprehension,
And the poore Beetle that we treade upon
In corporall sufferance, finds a pang as great,
As when a Giant dies.

Cla. But why give you me this shame?
Thinke you I can a resolution fetch
From flowrie tendernesse? If I must die,
I will encounter darknesse as a bride,
And hugge it in mine armes.

Isa. There spake my brother: there my fathers grave
Did utter forth a voice. Yes, thou must die:
Thou art too noble, to conserve a life
In base appliances. This outward sainted Deputie,
Whose setled visage, and deliberate word
Nips youth i'th head, and follies doth emmew
As Falcon doth the Fowle, is yet a divell:
His filth within being cast, he would appeare
A pond, as deepe as hell.

Cla. The prenzie, *Angelo*?

Isa. Oh 'tis the cunning Liverie of hell,
The damnest bodie to invest, and cover
In prenzie gardes; dost thou thinke *Claudio*,
If I would yeeld him my virginitie
Thou might'st be freed?

Cla. Oh heavens, it cannot be.

Isa. Yes, he would giv't thee; from this rank offence
So to offend him still. This night's the time
That I should do what I abhorre to name,
Or else thou diest to morrow.

Clau. Thou shalt not do't.

Isa. O, were it but my life,
I'de throw it downe for your deliverance
As frankely as a pin.

Clau. Thankes deere *Isabell*.

Isa. Be readie *Claudio*, for your death to morrow.

Clau. Yes. Has he affections in him,
That thus can make him bite the Law by th'nose,
When he would force it? Sure it is no sinne,
Or of the deadly seven it is the least.

Isa. Which is the least?

Cla. If it were damnable, he being so wise,
Why would he for the momentarie tricke
Be perdurablie fin'de? Oh *Isabell*.

Isa. What saies my brother?

Cla. Death is a feareful thing.

Isa. And shamed life, a hatefull.

Cla. I, but to die, and go we know not where,
To lie in cold obstruction, and to rot,
This sensible warme motion, to become
A kneaded clod; And the delighted spirit
To bath in fierie floods, or to recide
In thrilling Region of thicke-ribbed Ice,
To be imprison'd in the viewless windes
And blowne with restlesse violence round about
The pendant world: or to be worse then worst
Of those, that lawlesse and incertaine thought,

Imagine howling, 'tis too horrible.
The weariest, and most loathed worldly life
That Age, Ache, perjury, and imprisonment
Can lay on nature, is a Paradise
To what we feare of death.

   Isa. Alas, alas.

   Cla. Sweet Sister, let me live.
What sinne you do, to save a brothers life,
Nature dispenses with the deede so farre,
That it becomes a vertue.

   Isa. Oh you beast,
Oh faithlesse Coward, oh dishonest wretch,
Wilt thou be made a man, out of my vice?
Is't not a kinde of Incest, to take life
From thine owne sisters shame? What should I thinke,
Heaven shield my Mother plaid my Father faire:
For such a warped slip of wildernesse
Nere issu'd from his blood. Take my defiance,
Die, perish: Might but my bending downe
Repreeve thee from thy fate, it should proceede.
Ile pray a thousand praiers for thy death,
No word to save thee.

   Cla. Nay heare me *Isabell*.

   Isa. Oh fie, fie, fie;
Thy sinn's not accidentall, but a Trade;
Mercy to thee would prove it selfe a Bawd,
'Tis best that thou diest quickly.

   Cla. Oh heare me *Isabella*.

   Duk. Vouchsafe a word, yong sister, but one word.

   Isa. What is your Will.

   Duk. Might you dispense with your leysure, I would
by and by have some speech with you: the satisfaction I
would require, is likewise your owne benefit.

   Isa. I have no superflous leysure, my stay must be
stolen out of other affaires: but I will attend you a while.

   Duke. Son, I have over-heard what hath past between
you & your sister. *Angelo* had never the purpose to cor-

rupt her; onely he hath made an assay of her vertue, to
practise his judgement with the disposition of natures.
She (having the truth of honour in her) hath made him
that gracious deniall, which he is most glad to receive: I
am Confessor to *Angelo*, and I know this to be true, ther-
fore prepare your selfe to death: do not satisfie your resolution with hopes that are fallible, to morrow you
must die, goe to your knees, and make ready.

Cla. Let me ask my sister pardon, I am so out of love
with life, that I will sue to be rid of it.

Duke. Hold you there: farewell: *Provost*, a word
with you.

Pro. What's your will (father?)

Duk. That now you are come, you will be gone: leave
me a while with the Maid, my minde promises with my
habit, no losse shall touch her by my company.

Pro. In good time.   *Exit.*

Duk. The hand that hath made you faire, hath made
you good: the goodnes that is cheape in beauty, makes
beauty briefe in goodnes; but grace being the soule of
your complexion, shall keepe the body of it ever faire;
the assault that *Angelo* hath made to you, Fortune hath
convaid to my understanding; and but that frailty hath
examples for his falling, I should wonder at *Angelo*: how
will you doe to content this Substitute, and to save your
Brother?

Isab. I am now going to resolve him: I had rather
my brother die by the Law, then my sonne should be un-
lawfullie borne. But (oh) how much is the good Duke
deceiv'd in *Angelo*: if ever he returne, and I can speake
to him, I will open my lips in vaine, or discover his government.

Duke. That shall not be much amisse: yet, as the matter now stands, he will avoid your accusation: he made
triall of you onelie. Therefore fasten your eare on my
advisings, to the love I have in doing good; a remedie
presents it selfe. I doe make my selfe beleeve that you

may most uprighteously do a poor wronged Lady a me-
rited benefit; redeem your brother from the angry Law;
doe no staine to your owne gracious person, and much
please the absent Duke, if peradventure he shall ever returne to have hearing of this businesse.

Isab. Let me heare you speake farther; I have spirit to
do any thing that appeares not fowle in the truth of my
spirit.

Duke. Vertue is bold, and goodnes never fearefull:
Have you not heard speake of *Mariana* the sister of *Fredericke* the great Souldier, who miscarried at Sea?

Isa. I have heard of the Lady, and good words went
with her name.

Duke. Shee should this *Angelo* have married: was affianced to her oath, and the nuptiall appointed: between
which time of the contract, and limit of the solemnitie,
her brother *Fredericke* was wrackt at Sea, having in that
perished vessell, the dowry of his sister: but marke how
heavily this befell to the poore Gentlewoman, there she
lost a noble and renowned brother, in his love toward
her, ever most kinde and naturall: with him the portion
and sinew of her fortune, her marriage dowry: with
both, her combynate-husband, this well-seeming
Angelo.

Isab. Can this be so? did *Angelo* so leave her?

Duke. Left her in her teares, & dried not one of them
with his comfort: swallowed his vowes whole, preten-
ding in her, discoveries of dishonor: in few, bestow'd
her on her owne lamentation, which she yet weares for
his sake: and he, a marble to her teares, is washed with
them, but relents not.

Isab. What a merit were it in death to take this poore
maid from the world? what corruption in this life, that
it will let this man live? But how out of this can shee a-
vaile?

Duke. It is a rupture that you may easily heale: and the
cure of it not onely saves your brother, but keepes you

from dishonor in doing it.

Isab. Shew me how (good Father.)

Duk. This fore-named Maid hath yet in her the continuance of her first affection: his unjust unkindnesse
(that in all reason should have quenched her love) hath
(like an impediment in the Current) made it more vio-
lent and unruly: Goe you to *Angelo*, answere his requiring with a plausible obedience, agree with his demands
to the point: onely referre your selfe to this advantage;
first, that your stay with him may not be long: that the
time may have all shadow, and silence in it: and the place
answere to convenience: this being granted in course,
and now followes all: wee shall advise this wronged
maide to steed up your appointment, goe in your place:
if the encounter acknowledge it selfe heerafter, it may
compell him to her recompence; and heere, by this is
your brother saved, your honour untainted, the poore
Mariana advantaged, and the corrupt Deputy scaled.
The Maid will I frame, and make fit for his attempt: if
you thinke well to carry this as you may, the doublenes
of the benefit defends the deceit from reproofe. What
thinke you of it?

Isab. The image of it gives me content already, and I
trust it will grow to a most prosperous perfection.

Duk. It lies much in your holding up: haste you speedily to *Angelo*, if for this night he intreat you to his bed,
give him promise of satisfaction: I will presently to S.
Lukes, there at the moated-Grange recides this deje-
cted *Mariana*; at that place call upon me, and dispatch
with *Angelo*, that it may be quickly.

Isab. I thank you for this comfort: fare you well good
father.   *Exit.*

Enter Elbow, Clowne, Officers.

Elb. Nay, if there be no remedy for it, but that you
will needes buy and sell men and women like beasts, we
shall have all the world drinke browne & white bastard.

Measure, For Measure.

Duk. Oh heavens, what stuffe is heere.

Clow. Twas never merry world since of two usuries
the merriest was put downe, and the worser allow'd by
order of Law; a fur'd gowne to keepe him warme; and
furd with Foxe and Lamb-skins too, to signifie, that craft
being richer then Innocency, stands for the facing.

Elb. Come your way sir: 'blesse you good Father
Frier.

Duk. And you good Brother Father; what offence
hath this man made you, Sir?

Elb. Marry Sir, he hath offended the Law; and Sir,
we take him to be a Theefe too Sir: for wee have found
upon him Sir, a strange Pick-lock, which we have sent
to the Deputie.

Duke. Fie, sirrah, a Bawd, a wicked bawd,
The evill that thou causest to be done,
That is thy meanes to live. Do thou but thinke
What 'tis to cram a maw, or cloath a backe
From such a filthie vice: say to thy selfe,
From their abhominable and beastly touches
I drinke, I eate away my selfe, and live:
Canst thou beleeve thy living is a life,
So stinkingly depending? Go mend, go mend.

Clo. Indeed, it do's stinke in some sort, Sir:
But yet Sir I would proue.

Duke. Nay, if the divell have given thee proofs for sin
Thou wilt prove his. Take him to prison Officer:
Correction, and Instruction must both worke
Ere this rude beast will profit.

Elb. He must before the Deputy Sir, he ha's given
him warning: the Deputy cannot abide a Whore-ma-
ster: if he be a Whore-monger, and comes before him,
he were as good go a mile on his errand.

Duke. That we were all, as some would seeme to bee
From our faults, as faults from seeming free.

Enter Lucio.

[69]

Elb. His necke will come to your wast, a Cord sir.

Clo. I spy comfort, I cry baile: Here's a Gentleman,
and a friend of mine.

Luc. How now noble *Pompey*? What, at the wheels
Of *Casar*? Art thou led in triumph? What is there none
of *Pigmalions* Images newly made woman to bee had
now, for putting the hand in the pocket, and extracting
clutch'd? What reply? Ha? What saist thou to this
Tune, Matter, and Method? Is't not drown'd i'th last
raine? Ha? What saist thou Trot? Is the world as it was
Man? Which is the way? Is it sad, and few words?
Or how? The tricke of it?

Duke. Still thus, and thus: still worse?

Luc. How doth my deere Morsell, thy Mistris? Pro-
cures she still? Ha?

Clo. Troth sir, shee hath eaten up all her beefe, and
she is her selfe in the tub.

Luc. Why 'tis good: It is the right of it: it must be
so, Ever your fresh Whore, and your pouder'd Baud, an
unshun'd consequence, it must be so. Art going to prison *Pompey*?

Clo. Yes faith sir.

Luc. Why 'tis not amisse *Pompey*: farewell: goe say
I sent thee thether: for debt *Pompey*? Or how?

Elb. For being a baud, for being a baud.

Luc. Well, then imprison him: If imprisonment be
the due of a baud, why 'tis his right. Baud is he doubt-
lesse, and of antiquity too: Baud borne. Farewell good
Pompey: Commend me to the prison *Pompey*, you will
turne good husband now *Pompey*, you will keepe the
house.

Clo. I hope Sir, your good Worship wil be my baile?

Luc. No indeed wil I not *Pompey*, it is not the wear:
I will pray (*Pompey*) to encrease your bondage if you
take it not patiently: why, your mettle is the more:
Adieu trustie *Pompey*.
Blesse you Friar.

Duke. And you.

Luc. Do's *Bridget* paint still, *Pompey*? Ha?

Elb. Come your waies sir, come.

Clo. You will not baile me then Sir?

Luc. Then *Pompey*, nor now: what newes abroad *Fri-er*? What newes?

Elb. Come your waies sir, come.

Luc. Goe to kennell (*Pompey*) goe: What newes Frier of the Duke?

Duke. I know none: can you tell me of any?

Luc. Some say he is with the Emperor of *Russia*: other some, he is in *Rome*: but where is he thinke you?

Duke. I know not where: but wheresoever, I wish him well.

Luc. It was a mad fantasticall tricke of him to steale from the State, and usurpe the beggerie hee was never borne to: Lord *Angelo* Dukes it well in his absence: he puts transgression too't.

Duke. He do's well in't.

Luc. A little more lenitie to Lecherie would doe no harme in him: Something too crabbed that way, *Frier*.

Duk. It is too general a vice, and severitie must cure it.

Luc. Yes in good sooth, the vice is of a great kindred; it is well allied, but it is impossible to extirpe it quite, Frier, till eating and drinking be put downe. They say this *Angelo* was not made by Man and Woman, after this downe-right way of Creation: is it true, thinke you?

Duke. How should he be made then?

Luc. Some report, a Sea-maid spawn'd him. Some, that he was begot betweene two Stock-fishes. But it is certaine, that when he makes water, his Urine is con-geal'd ice, that I know to bee true: and he is a motion generative, that's infallible.

Duke. You are pleasant sir, and speake apace.

Luc. Why, what a ruthlesse thing is this in him, for the rebellion of a Cod-peece, to take away the life of a

man? Would the *Duke* that is absent have done this?
Ere he would have hang'd a man for the getting a hundred Bastards, he would have paide for the Nursing a
thousand. He had some feeling of the sport, hee knew
the service, and that instructed him to mercie.

Duke. I never heard the absent *Duke* much detected
for Women, he was not enclin'd that way.

Luc. Oh Sir, you are deceiv'd.

Duke. 'Tis not possible.

Luc. Who, not the Duke? Yes, your beggar of fifty:
and his use was, to put a ducket in her Clack-dish; the
Duke had Crochets in him. Hee would be drunke too,
that let me informe you.

Duke. You do him wrong, surely.

Luc. Sir, I was an inward of his: a shie fellow was
the Duke, and I beleeve I know the cause of his with-
drawing.

Duke. What (I prethee) might be the cause?

Luc. No, pardon: 'Tis a secret must bee lockt within the teeth and the lippes: but this I can let you understand, the greater file of the subject held the *Duke* to be
wise.

Duke. Wise? Why no question but he was.

Luc. A very superficiall, ignorant, unweighing fellow

Duke. Either this is Envie in you, Folly, or mista-
king: The very streame of his life, and the businesse he
hath helmed, must uppon a warranted neede, give him
a better proclamation. Let him be but testimonied in
his owne bringings forth, and hee shall appeare to the
envious, a Scholler, a Statesman, and a Soldier: therefore you speake unskilfully: or, if your knowledge bee
more, it is much darkned in your malice.

Luc. Sir, I know him, and I love him.

Duke. Love talkes with better knowldege,& knowledge with deare love.

Luc. Come Sir, I know what I know.

Duke. I can hardly beleeve that, since you know not

what you speake. But if ever the *Duke* returne (as our
praiers are he may) let mee desire you to make your answer before him: if it bee honest you have spoke, you
have courage to maintaine it; I am bound to call uppon
you, and I pray you your name?

Luc. Sir my name is *Lucio*, wel known to the Duke.

Duke. He shall know you better Sir, if I may live to
report you.

Luc. I feare you not.

Duke. O, you hope the *Duke* will returne no more:
or you imagine me to unhurtfull an opposite: but indeed
I can doe you little harme: You'll for-sweare this a-
gaine?

Luc. Ile be hang'd first: Thou art deceiv'd in mee
Friar. But no more of this: Canst thou tell if *Claudio*
die to morrow, or no?

Duke. Why should he die Sir?

Luc. Why? For filling a bottle with a Tunne-dish:
I would the Duke we talke of were return'd againe: this
ungenitur'd Agent will un-people the Province with
Continencie. Sparrowes must not build in his house-
eeves, because they are lecherous: The *Duke* yet would
have darke deeds darkelie answered, hee would never
bring them to light: would hee were return'd. Marrie
this *Claudio* is condemned for untrussing. Farewell good
Friar, I prethee pray for me: The *Duke* (I say to thee
againe) would eate Mutton on Fridaies. He's now past
it, yet (and I say to thee) hee would mouth with a beggar, though she smelt browne-bread and Garlicke: say
that I said so: Farewell.   *Exit.*

Duke. No might, nor greatnesse in mortality
Can censure scape: Back-wounding calumnie
The whitest vertue strikes. What King so strong,
Can tie the gall up in the slanderous tong?
But who comes heere?

Enter Escalus, Provost, and Bawd.

[73]

Esc. Go, away with her to prison.

Bawd. Good my Lord be good to mee, your Honor is accounted a mercifull man: good my Lord.

Esc. Double, and trebble admonition, and still for-feite in the same kinde? This would make mercy sweare and play the Tirant.

Pro. A Bawd of eleven yeares continuance, may it please your Honor.

Bawd. My Lord, this is one *Lucio's* information a-gainst me, Mistris *Kate Keepe-downe* was with childe by him in the Dukes time, he promis'd her marriage: his Childe is a yeere and a quarter olde come *Philip* and *Ja-cob*: I have kept it my selfe; and see how hee goes about to abuse me.

Esc. That fellow is a fellow of much License: Let him be call'd before us. Away with her to prison: Goe too, no more words. Provost, my Brother *Angelo* will not be alter'd, *Claudio* must die to morrow: Let him be furnish'd with Divines, and have all charitable prepara-tion. If my brother wrought by my pitie, it should not be so with him.

Pro. So please you, this Friar hath beene with him, and advis'd him for th'entertainment of death.

Esc. Good'even, good Father.

Duke. Blisse, and goodnesse on you.

Esc. Of whence are you?

Duke. Not of this Countrie, though my chance is now To use it for my time: I am a brother Of gracious Order, late come from the Sea, In speciall businesse from his Holinesse.

Esc. What newes abroad i'th World?

Duke. None, but that there is so great a Feavor on goodnesse, that the dissolution of it must cure it. No-veltie is onely in request, and as it is as dangerous to be aged in any kinde of course, as it is vertuous to be con-stant in any undertaking. There is scarce truth enough alive to make Societies secure, but Securitie enough to

make Fellowships accurst: Much upon this riddle runs
the wisedome of the world: This newes is old enough,
yet it is everie daies newes. I pray you Sir, of what disposition was the Duke?

Esc. One, that above all other strifes,
Contended especially to know himselfe.

Duke. What pleasure was he given to?

Esc. Rather rejoycing to see another merry, then
merrie at anie thing which profest to make him rejoice.
A Gentleman of all temperance. But leave wee him to
his events, with a praier they may prove prosperous, &
let me desire to know, how you finde *Claudio* prepar'd?
I am made to understand, that you have lent him visita-
tion.

Duke. He professes to have received no sinister measure from his Judge, but most willingly humbles himselfe to the determination of Justice: yet had he framed
to himselfe (by the instruction of his frailty) manie de-
ceyving promises of life, which I (by my good leisure)
have discredited to him, and now is he resolv'd to die.

Esc. You have paid the heavens your Function, and
the prisoner the verie debt of your Calling. I have labour'd for the poore Gentleman, to the extremest shore
of my modestie, but my brother-Justice have I found so
severe, that he hath forc'd me to tell him, hee is indeede
Justice.

Duke. If his owne life,
Answere the straitnesse of his proceeding,
It shall become him well: wherein if he chance to faile
he hath sentenc'd himselfe.

Esc. I am going to visit the prisoner, Fare you well.

Duke. Peace be with you.
He who the sword of Heaven will beare,
Should be as holy, as seveare:
Patterne in himselfe to know,
Grace to stand, and Vertue go:
More, nor lesse to others paying,

Then by selfe-offences weighing.
Shame to him, whose cruell striking,
Kils for faults of his owne liking:
Twice trebble shame on *Angelo*,
To weede my vice, and let his grow.
Oh, what may Man within him hide,
Though Angel on the outward side?
How may likenesse made in crimes,
Making practise on the Times,
To draw with ydle Spiders strings
Most ponderous and substantiall things?
Craft against vice, I must applie.
With *Angelo* to night shall lye
His old betroathed (but despised:)
So disguise shall by th'disguised
Pay with falshood, false exacting,
And performe an olde contracting.   *Exit*

Actus Quartus. Scoena Prima.

Enter Mariana, and Boy singing.

Song.   *Take, oh take those lips away,*
               that so sweetly were forsworne,
           And those eyes: the breake of day
               lights that doe mislead the Morne;
           But my kisses bring againe, bring againe,
           Seales of love, but seal'd in vaine, seal'd in vaine.

Enter Duke.

  Mar. Breake off thy song, and haste thee quick away,
Here comes a man of comfort, whose advice
Hath often still'd my brawling discontent.
I cry you mercie, Sir, and well could wish
You had not found me here so musicall.
Let me excuse me, and beleeve me so,
My mirth it much displeas'd, but pleas'd my woe.

[76]

Duk. 'Tis good; though Musick oft hath such a charme
To make bad, good; and good provoake to harme.
I pray you tell me, hath any body enquir'd for mee here
to day; much upon this time have I promis'd here to
meete.

Mar. You have not bin enquir'd after: I have sat
here all day.

Enter Isabell.

Duk. I doe constantly beleeve you: the time is come
even now. I shall crave your forbearance alittle, may be
I will call upon you anone for some advantage to your
selfe.

Mar. I am alwayes bound to you.   *Exit.*

Duk. Very well met, and well come:
What is the newes from this good Deputie?

Isab. He hath a Garden circummur'd with Bricke.
Whose westerne side is with a Vineyard back't;
And to that Vineyard is a planched gate,
That makes his opening with this bigger Key:
This other doth command a little doore,
Which from the Vineyard to the Garden leades,
There have I made my promise, upon the
Heavy midle of the night, to call upon him.

Duk. But shall you on your knowledge find this way?

Isab. I have t'ane a due, and wary note upon't,
With whispering, and most guiltie diligence,
In action all of precept, he did show me
The way twice ore.

Duk. Are there no other tokens
Betweene you 'greed, concerning her observance?

Isab. No: none but onely a repaire ith' darke,
And that I have possest him, my most stay
Can be but briefe: for I have made him know,
I have a Servant comes with me along
That staies upon me; whose perswasion is,
I come about my Brother.

[77]

Duk. 'Tis well borne up.
I have not yet made knowne to *Mariana*

Enter Mariana.

A word of this: what hoa, within; come forth,
I pray you be acquainted with this Maid,
She comes to doe you good.
    Isab. I doe desire the like.
    Duk. Do you perswade your selfe that I respect you?
    Mar. Good Frier, I know you do, and have found it.
    Duke. Take then this your companion by the hand
Who hath a storie readie for your eare:
I shall attend your leisure, but make haste
The vaporous night approaches.
    Mar. Wilt please you walke aside.   *Exit.*
    Duke. Oh Place, and greatnes: millions of false eies
Are stucke upon thee: volumes of report
Run with these false, and most contrarious Quest
Upon thy doings: thousand escapes of wit
Make thee the father of their idle dreame,
And racke thee in their fancies. Welcome, how agreed?

Enter Mariana and Isabella.

    Isab. She'll take the enterprize upon her father,
If you advise it.
    Duke. It is not my consent,
But my entreaty too.
    Isab. Little have you to say
When you depart from him, but soft and low,
Remember now my brother.
    Mar. Feare me not.
    Duk. Nor gentle daughter, feare you not at all:
He is your husband on a pre-contract:
To bring you thus together 'tis no sinne,
Sith that the Justice of your title to him
Doth flourish the deceit. Come, let us goe,
Our Corne's to reape, for yet our Tithes to sow.   *Exeunt.*

Measure, For Measure.
Scena Secunda.

Enter Provost and Clowne.

Pro. Come hither sirha; can you cut off a mans head?
Clo. If the man be a Bachelor Sir, I can:
But if he be a married man, he's his wives head,
And I can never cut off a womans head.

Pro. Come sir, leave your snatches, and yeeld mee
a direct answere. To morrow morning are to die *Claudio* and *Barnardine*: heere is in our prison a common executioner, who in his office lacks a helper, if you will take
it on you to assist him, it shall redeeme you from your
Gyves: if not, you shall have our full time of imprisonment, and your deliverance with an unpittied whipping;
for you have beene a notorious bawd.

Clo. Sir, I have beene an unlawfull bawd, time out of
minde, but yet I will bee content to be a lawfull hang-
man: I would bee glad to receive some instruction from
my fellow partner.

Pro. What hoa, *Abhorson*: where's *Abhorson* there?

Enter Abhorson.

Abh. Doe you call sir?
Pro. Sirha, here's a fellow will helpe you to morrow
in your execution: if you thinke it meet, compound with
him by the yeere, and let him abide here with you, if not,
use him for the present, and dismisse him, hee cannot
plead his estimation with you: he hath beene a Bawd.

Abh. A Bawd Sir? fie upon him, he will discredit our
mysterie.

Pro. Goe too Sir, you waigh equallie: a feather will
turne the Scale.   *Exit.*

Clo. Pray sir, by your good favor: for surely sir, a
good favor you have, but that you have a hanging look:
Doe you call sir, your occupation a Mysterie?

Abh. I Sir, a Misterie.

[79]

Clo. Painting Sir, I have heard say, is a Misterie; and your Whores sir, being members of my occupation, u-sing painting, do prove my Occupation, a Misterie: but what Misterie there should be in hanging, if I should be hang'd, I cannot imagine.

Abh. Sir, it is a Misterie.

Clo. Proofe.

Abh. Everie true mans apparell fits your Theefe.

Clo. If it be too little for your theefe, your true man thinkes it bigge enough. If it bee too bigge for your Theefe, your Theefe thinkes it little enough: So everie true mans apparell fits your Theefe.

Enter Provost.

Pro. Are you agreed?

Clo. Sir, I will serve him: For I do finde your Hang-man is a more penitent Trade then your Bawd: he doth oftener aske forgivenesse.

Pro. You sirrah, provide your blocke and your Axe to morrow, foure a clocke.

Abh. Come on (Bawd) I will instruct thee in my Trade: follow.

Clo. I do desire to learne sir: and I hope, if you have occasion to use me for your owne turne, you shall finde me y'are. For truly sir, for your kindnesse, I owe you a good turne.   *Exit*

Pro. Call hether *Barnardine* and *Claudio*:
Th'one has my pitie; not a jot the other,
Being a Murtherer, though he were my brother.

Enter Claudio.

Looke, here's the Warrant *Claudio*, for thy death,
'Tis now dead midnight, and by eight to morrow
Thou must be made immortall. Where's *Barnadine*?

Cla. As fast lock'd up in sleepe, as guiltlesse labour,
When it lies starkely in the Travellers bones,
He will not wake.

Pro. Who can do good on him?
Well, go, prepare your selfe. But harke, what noise?
Heaven give your spirits comfort: by, and by,
I hope it is some pardon, or repreeve
For the most gentle *Claudio.* Welcome Father.

Enter Duke.

Duke. The best, and wholsomst spirits of the night,
Invellop you, good Provost: who call'd heere of late?
Pro. None since the Curphew rung.
Duke. Not *Isabell*?
Pro. No.
Duke. They will then er't be long.
Pro. What comfort is for *Claudio*?
Duke. There's some in hope.
Pro. It is a bitter Deputie.
Duke. Not so, not so: his life is paralel'd
Even with the stroke and line of his great Justice:
He doth with holie abstinence subdue
That in himselfe, which he spurres on his powre
To qualifie in others: were he meal'd with that
Which he corrects, then were he tirrannous,
But this being so, he's just. Now are they come.
This is a gentle Provost, sildome when
The steeled Gaoler is the friend of men:
How now? what noise? That spirit's possest with hast,
That wounds th'unsisting Posterne with these strokes.
Pro. There he must stay until the Officer
Arise to let him in: he is call'd up.
Duke. Have you no countermand for *Claudio* yet?
But he must die tomorrow?
Pro. None Sir, none.
Duke. As neere the dawning Provost, as it is,
You shall heare more ere Morning.
Pro. Happely
You something know: yet I beleeve there comes
No countermand: no such example have we:

[81]

Besides, upon the verie siege of Justice,
Lord *Angelo* hath to the publicke eare
Profest the contrarie.

Enter a Messenger.

  Duke. This is his Lords man.
  Pro. And heere comes *Claudio*'s pardon.
  Mess. My Lord hath sent you this note,
And by mee this further charge;
That you swerve not from the smallest Article of it,
Neither in time, matter, or other circumstance.
Good morrow: for as I take it, it is almost day.
  Pro. I shall obey him.
  Duke. This is his Pardon purchas'd by such sin,
For which the Pardoner himselfe is in:
Hence hath offence his quicke celeritie,
When it is borne in high Authority.
When Vice makes Mercie; Mercie's so extended,
That for the faults love, is th'offender friended.
Now Sir, what newes?
  Pro. I told you:
Lord *Angelo* (be-like) thinking me remisse
In mine Office, awakens mee
With this unwonted putting on, methinks strangely:
For he hath not us'd it before.
  Duk. Pray you let's heare.

The Letter.

*Whatsoever you may heare to the contrary, let Claudio be ex-
ecuted by foure of the clocke, and in the afternoone Bernar-
dine: For my better satisfaction, let mee have Claudios
head sent me by five. Let this be duely performed with a
thought that more depends on it, then we must yet deliver.
Thus faile not to doe your Office, as you will answere it at
your perill.*
What say you to this Sir?
  Duke. What is that *Barnardine*, who is to be executed in th'afternoone?

Pro. A Bohemian borne: But here nurst up & bred,
One that is a prisoner nine yeeres old.

Duke. How came it, that the absent *Duke* had not
either deliver'd him to his libertie, or executed him? I
have heard it was ever his manner to do so.

Pro. His friends still wrought Repreeves for him:
And indeed his fact till now in the government of Lord
Angelo, came not to an undoubtfull proofe.

Duke. Is it now apparant?

Pro. Most manifest, and not denied by himselfe.

Duke. Hath he borne himselfe penitently in prison?
How seems he to be touch'd?

Pro. A man that apprehends death no more dread-
fully, but as a drunken sleepe, careless, wreaklesse, and
fearelesse of what's past, present, or to come: insensible
of mortality, and desperately mortall.

Duke. He wants advice.

Pro. He will heare none: he hath evermore had the liberty of the prison: give him leave to escape hence, hee
would not. Drunke many times a day, if not many daies
entirely drunke. We have verie oft awak'd him, as if to
carrie him to execution, and shew'd him a seeming warrant for it, it hath not moved him at all.

Duke. More of him anon: There is written in your
brow Provost, honesty and constancie; if I reade it not
truly, my ancient skill beguiles me: but in the boldnes
of my cunning, I will lay my selfe in hazard: *Claudio*,
whom heere you have warrant to execute, is no greater
forfeit to the Law, then *Angelo* who hath sentenc'd him.
To make you understand this in a manifested effect, I
crave but foure daies respit: for the which, you are to
do me both a present, and a dangerous courtesie.

Pro. Pray Sir, in what?

Duke. In the delaying death.

Pro. Alacke, how may I do it? Having the houre limited, and an expresse command, under penaltie, to deliver his head in the view of *Angelo*? I may make my

case as *Claudio's*, to cross this in the smallest.

 Duke. By the vow of mine Order, I warrant you,
If my instructions may be your guide,
Let this *Barnardine* be this morning executed,
And his head borne to *Angelo.*

 Pro. Angelo hath seene them both,
And will discover the favour.

 Duke. Oh death's a great disguiser, and you may
adde to it; Shave the head, and tie the beard, and say it
was the desire of the penitent to be so bar'de before his
death: you know the course is common. If any thing
fall to you upon this, more then thankes and good fortune, by the Saint whom I professe, I will plead against
it with my life.

 Pro. Pardon me, good Father, it is against my oath.

 Duke. Were you sworne to the Duke, or to the Deputie?

 Pro. To him, and to his Substitutes.

 Duke. You will thinke you have made no offence, if
the *Duke* avouch the justice of your dealing?

 Pro. But what likelihood is in that?

 Duke. Not a resemblance, but a certainty; yet since
I see you fearfull, that neither my coate, integrity, nor
perswasion, can with ease attempt you, I will go further
then I meant, to plucke all feares out of you. Looke
you Sir, heere is the hand and Seale of the Duke : you
know the Character I doubt not, and the Signet is not
strange to you?

 Pro. I know them both.

 Duke. The Contents of this, is the returne of the
Duke: you shall anon over-reade it at your pleasure:
where you shall finde within these two daies, he wil be
heere. This is a thing that *Angelo* knowes not, for hee
this very day receives letters of strange tenor, perchance
of the Dukes death, perchance entering into some Mo-
nasterie, but by chance nothing of what is writ. Looke,
th'unfolding Starre calles up the Shepheard; put not

your selfe into amazement, how these things should be; all difficulties are but easie when they are knowne. Call your executioner, and off with *Barnardines* head: I will give him a present shrift, and advise him for a better place. Yet you are amaz'd, but this shall absolutely re-solve you: Come away, it is almost cleere dawne. *Exit.*

Scena Tertia.

Enter Clowne.

Clo. I am as well acquainted heere, as I was in our house of profession: one would thinke it were Mistris *Over-dons* owne house, for heere be manie of her olde Customers. First, here's yong Mr *Rash*, hee's in for a commoditie of browne paper, and olde Ginger, nine score and seventeene pounds, of which hee made five Markes readie money: marrie then, Ginger was not much in request, for the olde Women were all dead. Then is there heere one Mr *Caper*, at the suite of Master *Three-Pile* the Mercer, for some foure suites of Peach-colour'd Satten, which now peaches him a beggar. Then have we heere, yong *Dizie*, and yong Mr *Deepe-vow*, and Mr *Copperspurre*, and Mr *Starve-Lackey* the Ra-pier and dagger man, and yong *Drop-heire* that kild lu-stie *Pudding*, and Mr *Forthlight* the Tilter, and brave Mr *Shootie* the great Traveller, and wilde *Halfe-Canne* that stabb'd Pots, and I thinke fortie more, all great doers in our Trade, and are now for the Lords sake.

Enter Abhorson.

Abh. Sirrah, bring *Barnardine* hether.
Clo. Mr *Barnardine*, you must rise and be hang'd, Mr *Barnardine*.
Abh. What hoa *Barnardine*.

Barnardine within.

Bar. A pox o'your throats: who makes that noyse there? What are you?

Clo. Your friends Sir, the Hangman:
You must be so good Sir to rise, and be put to death.

Bar. Away you Rogue, away, I am sleepie.

Abh. Tell him he must awake,
And that quickly too.

Clo. Pray Master *Barnardine*, awake till you are ex-exuted, and sleepe afterwards.

Ab. Go in to him, and fetch him out.

Clo. He is comming Sir, he is comming: I heare his Straw russle.

Enter Barnadine.

Abh. Is the Axe upon the blocke, sirrah?

Clo. Verie readie Sir.

Bar. How now *Abhorson*?
What's the newes with you?

Abh. Truly Sir, I would desire you to clap into your prayers: for looke you, the Warrants come.

Bar. You Rogue, I have bin drinking all night,
I am not fitted for't.

Clo. Oh, the better Sir: for he that drinkes all night, and is hanged betimes in the morning, may sleepe the sounder all the next day.

Enter Duke.

Abh. Looke you Sir, heere comes your ghostly Father: do we jest now thinke you?

Duke. Sir, induced by my charitie, and hearing how hastily you are to depart, I am come to advise you, Comfort you, and pray with you.

Bar. Friar, not I: I have bin drinking hard all night, and I will have more time to prepare mee, or they shall beat out my braines with billets: I will not consent to die this day, that's certaine.

Duke. Oh sir, you must: and therefore I beseech you

Looke forward on the journie you shall go.

Bar. I sweare I will not die to day for anie mans perswasion.

Duke. But heare you:

Bar. Not a word: if you have anie thing to say to me,
come to my Ward: for thence will not I to day.

Exit

Enter Provost.

Duke. Unfit to live, or die: oh gravell heart.
After him (Fellowes) bring him to the blocke.

Pro. Now Sir, how do you finde the prisoner?

Duke. A creature unpre-par'd, unmeet for death,
And to transport him in the minde he is,
Were damnable.

Pro. Heere in the prison, Father,
There died this morning of a cruell Feavor,
One *Ragozine*, a most notorious Pirate,
A man of *Claudio*'s yeares: his beard, and head
Just of his colour. What if we do omit
This Reprobate, til he were wel enclin'd,
And satisfie the Deputie with the visage
Of *Ragozine*, more like to *Claudio*?

Duke. Oh,'tis an accident that heaven provides:
Dispatch it presently, the houre drawes on
Prefixt by *Angelo*: See this be done,
And sent according to command, whiles I
Perswade this rude wretch willingly to die.

Pro. This shall be done (good Father) presently:
But *Barnardine* must die this afternoone,
And how shall we continue *Claudio*,
To save me from the danger that might come,
If he were knowne alive?

Duke. Let this be done,
Put them in secret holds, both *Barnardine* and *Claudio*,
Ere twice the sun hath made his journall greeting
To yond generation, you shal finde

[87]

Your safetie manifested.

    Pro. I am your free dependant.   *Exit.*

    Duke. Quicke, dispatch, and send the head to *Angelo*
Now will I write Letters to *Angelo*,
(The Provost he shal beare them) whose contents
Shal witnesse to him I am neere at home:
And that by great Injunctions I am bound
To enter publikely: him Ile desire
To meet me at the consecrated Fount,
A League below the Citie: and from thence,
By cold gradation, and weale-ballanc'd forme.
We shal proceed with *Angelo.*

Enter Provost.

    Pro. Heere is the head, Ile carrie it my selfe.

    Duke. Convenient is it: Make a swift returne,
For I would commune with you of such things,
That want no eare but yours.

    Pro. Ile make all speede.   *Exit*

Isabell within.

    Isa. Peace hoa, be heere.

    Duke. The tongue of *Isabell.* She's come to know,
If yet her brothers pardon be come hither:
But I will keepe her ignorant of her good,
To make her heavenly comforts of dispaire,
When it is least expected.

Enter Isabella.

    Isa. Hoa, by your leave.

    Duke. Good morning to you, faire, and gracious
daughter.

    Isa. The better given me by so holy a man,
Hath yet the Deputie sent my brothers pardon?

    Duke. He hath releasd him, *Isabell*, from the world,
His head is off, and sent to *Angelo.*

    Isa. Nay, but it is not so.

    Duke. It is no other,

Shew your wisedome daughter in your close patience.

    Isa. Oh, I wil to him, and plucke out his eies.

    Duk. You shal not be admitted to his sight.

    Isa. Unhappie *Claudio*, wretched *Isabell*,
Injurious world, most damned *Angelo*.

    Duke. This nor hurts him, nor profits you a jot,
Forbeare it therefore, give your cause to heaven,
Marke what I say, which you shal finde
By every sillable a faithful veritie.
The Duke comes home to morrow: nay drie your eyes,
One of our Covent, and his Confessor
Gives me this instance: Already he hath carried
Notice to *Escalus* and *Angelo*,
Who do prepare to meete him at the gates,
There to give up their powre: If you can pace your wisdome,
In that good path that I would wish it go,
And you shal have your bosome on this wretch,
Grace of the Duke, revenges to your heart,
And general Honor.

    Isa. I am directed by you.

    Duk. This Letter then to Friar *Peter* give,
'Tis that he sent me of the Dukes returne:
Say, by this token, I desire his companie
At *Mariana*'s house to night. Her cause, and yours
Ile perfect him withall, and he shal bring you
Before the Duke; and to the head of *Angelo*
Accuse him home and home. For my poore selfe,
I am combined by a sacred Vow,
And shall be absent. Wend you with this Letter:
Command these fretting waters from your eies
With a light heart; trust not my holie Order
If I pervert your course: whose heere?

               Enter Lucio.

    Luc. Good'even;
Frier, where's the Provost?

    Duke. Not within Sir.

Luc. Oh prettie *Isabella*, I am pale at mine heart, to
see thine eyes so red: thou must be patient; I am faine
to dine and sup with water and bran: I dare not for my
head fill my belly. One fruitful Meale would set mee
too't: but they say the *Duke* will be heere to Morrow.
By my troth *Isabell* I lov'd thy brother, if the olde fan-
tastical *Duke* of darke corners had bene at home, he had
lived.

Duke. Sir, the Duke is marveilous little beholding
to your reports, but the best is, he lives not in them.

Luc. Friar, thou knowest not the Duke so wel as I
do: he's a better woodman then thou tak'st him for.

Duke. Well: you'l answer this one day. Fare you well.

Luc. Nay tarrie, Ile go along with thee,
I can tel thee pretty tales of the Duke.

Duke. You have told me too many of him already sir
if they be true: if not true, none were enough.

Lucio. I was once before him for getting a Wench
with childe.

Duke. Did you such a thing?

Luc. Yes marrie did I; but I was faine to forswear it,
They would else have married me to the rotten Medler.

Duke. Sir your company is fairer then honest, rest you
well.

Luc. By my troth Ile go with thee to the lanes end:
if baudy talke offend you, we'el have very little of it: nay
Friar, I am a kind of Burre, I shal sticke.   *Exeunt*

Scena Quarta.

Enter Angelo & Escalus.

Esc. Every Letter he hath writ, hath disvouch'd other.

An. In most uneven and distracted manner, his actions
show much like to madnesse, pray heaven his wisedome
bee not tainted: and why meet him at the gates and re-

liver ou rauthorities there?

Esc. I ghesse not.

Ang. And why should wee proclaime it in an howre
before his entring, that if any crave redresse of injustice,
they should exhibit their petitions in the street?

Esc. He showes his reason for that: to have a dispatch
of Complaints, and to deliver us from devices heere-
after, which shall then have no power to stand against
us.

Ang. Well: I beseech you let it bee proclaim'd betimes i'th' morne, Ile call you at your house: give notice
to such men of sort and suite as are to meete him.

Esc. I shall sir: fare you well. *Exit.*

Ang. Good night.
This deede unshapes me quite, makes me unpregnant
And dull to all proceedings. A deflowred maid,
And by an eminent body, that enforc'd
The Law against it? But that her tender shame
Will not proclaime against her maiden losse,
How might she tongue me? yet reason dares her no,
For my Authority beares of a credent bulke,
That no particular scandall once can touch
But it confounds the breather. He should have liv'd,
Save that his riotous youth with dangerous sense
Might in the times to come have ta'ne revenge
By so receiving a dishonor'd life
With ransome of such shame: would yet he had lived.
Alack, when once our grace we have forgot,
Nothing goes right, we would, and we would not. *Exit.*

Scena Quinta.

Enter Duke and Frier Peter.

Duke. These Letters at fit time deliver me.
The Provost knowes our purpose and our plot,

[91]

The matter being a foote, keepe your instruction
And hold you ever to our speciall drift,
Though sometimes you doe blench from this to that
As cause doth minister: Goe call at *Flavia*'s house,
And tell him where I stay: give the like notice
To *Valencius*, *Rowland*, and to *Crassus*,
And bid them bring the Trumpets to the gate:
But send me *Flavius* first.
    Peter. It shall be speeded well.

Enter Varrius.

    Duke. I thank thee *Varrius*, thou hast made good hast,
Come, we will walke: There's other of our friends
Will greet us heere anon: my gentle *Varrius*.   *Exeunt*.

Scena Sexta.

Enter Isabella and Mariana.

    Isab. To speak so indirectly I am loath,
I would say the truth, but to accuse him so
That is your part, yet I am advis'd to doe it,
He saies, to vaile full purpose.
    Mar. Be rul'd by him.
    Isab. Besides he tells me, that if peradventure
He speake against me on the adverse side,
I should not thinke it strange, for 'tis a physicke
That's bitter, to sweet end.

Enter Peter.

    Mar. I would *Frier Peter*
    Isab. Oh peace, the *Frier* is come.
    Peter. Come I have found you a stand most fit,
Where you may have such vantage on the *Duke*
He shall not passe you:
Twice have the Trumpets sounded.

[92]

The generous, and gravest Citizens
Have hent the gates, and very neere upon
The *Duke* is entring:
Therefore hence away.   *Exeunt.*

Actus Quintus. Scoena Prima.

Enter Duke, Varrius, Lords, Angelo, Esculus, Lucio,
Citizens at severall doores.

   Duk. My very worthy Cosen, fairely met,
Our old, and faithfull friend, we are glad to see you.
   Ang. Esc. Happy returne be to your royall grace.
   Duke. Many and harty thankings to you both:
We have made enquiry of you, and we heare
Such goodnesse of your Justice, that our soule
Cannot but yeeld you forth to publique thankes
Forerunning more requitall.
   Ang. You make my bonds still greater.
   Duk. Oh your desert speaks loud, & I should wrong it
To locke it in the wards of covert bosome
When it deserves with characters of brasse
A forted residence 'gainst the tooth of time,
And razure of oblivion: Give we your hand
And let the Subject see, to make them know
That outward curtesies would faine proclaime
Favours that keepe within: Come *Escalus,*
You must walke by us, on our other hand:
And good supporters are you.

                 Enter Peter and Isabella.

   Peter. Now is your time
Speake loud, and kneele before him.
   Isab. Justice, O royall *Duke,* vaile your regard
Upon a wrong'd (I would faine have said a Maid)
Oh worthy Prince, dishonor not your eye

                         [93]

By throwing it on any other object,
Till you have heard me, in my true complaint,
And given me Justice, Justice, Justice, Justice.

    Duk. Relate your wrongs;
In what, by whom? be briefe:
Here is Lord *Angelo* shall give you Justice,
Reveale your selfe to him.

    Isab. Oh worthy *Duke*,
You bid me seeke redemption of the divell,
Heare me your selfe: for that which I must speake
Must either punish me, not being beleev'd,
Or wring redresse from you:
Heare me: oh heare me, heere.

    Ang. My Lord, her wits I feare me are not firme:
She hath bin a suitor to me, for her Brother
Cut off by course of Justice.

    Isab. By course of Justice.

    Ang. And she will speake most bitterly, and strange.

    Isab. Most strange: but yet most truely wil I speake,
That *Angelo*'s forsworne, is it not strange?
That *Angelo*'s a murtherer, is't not strange?
That *Angelo* is an adulterous thiefe,
An hypocrite, a virgin violator,
Is it not strange? and strange?

    Duke. Nay it is ten times strange?

    Isa. It is not truer he is *Angelo*,
Then this is all as true, as it is strange;
Nay, it is ten times true, for truth is truth
To th'end of reckning.

    Duke. Away with her: poore soule
She speakes this, in th'infirmity of sence.

    Isa. Oh Prince, I conjure thee, as thou beleev'st
There is another comfort, then this world,
That thou neglect me not, with that opinion
That I am touch'd with madnesse: make not impossible
That which but seemes unlike, 'tis not impossible
But one, the wickedst caitiffe on the ground

May seeme as shie, as grave, as just, as absolute:
As *Angelo*, even so may *Angelo*
In all his dressings, caracts, titles, formes,
Be an arch-villaine: Beleeve it, royall Prince
If he be lesse, he's nothing, but he's more,
Had I more name for badnesse.

   Duke. By mine honesty
If she be mad, as I beleeve no other,
Her madnesse hath the oddest frame of sense,
Such a dependancy of thing, on thing,
As ere I heard in madnesse.

   Isab. Oh gracious *Duke*
Harpe not on that; nor do not banish reason
For inequality, but let your reason serve
To make the truth appeare, where it seemes hid,
And hide the false seemes true.

   Duk. Many that are not mad
Have sure more lacke of reason:
What would you say?

   Isab. I am the Sister of one *Claudio*,
Condemnd upon the Act of Fornication
To loose his head, condemn'd by *Angelo*,
I, (in probation of a Sisterhood)
Was sent to by my Brother; one *Lucio*
As then the Messenger.

   Luc. That's I, and't like your Grace:
I came to her from *Claudio*, and desir'd her,
To try her gracious fortune with Lord *Angelo*,
For her poore Brothers pardon.

   Isab. That's he indeede.

   Duk. You were not bid to speake.

   Luc. No, my good Lord,
Nor wish'd to hold my peace.

   Duk. I wish you now then,
Pray you take note of it: and when you have
A businesse for your selfe: pray heaven you then
Be perfect.

Luc. I warrant your honor.

Duk. The warrant's for your selfe: take heede to't.

Isab. This Gentleman told somewhat of my Tale.

Luc. Right.

Duk. It may be right, but you are i'the wrong
To speake before your time: proceed,

Isab. I went
To this pernicious Caitiffe Deputie.

Duk. That's somewhat madly spoken.

Isab. Pardon it,
The phrase is to the matter.

Duke. Mended againe: the matter: proceed.

Isab. In briefe, to set the needlesse processe by:
How I perswaded, how I praid, and kneel'd,
How he refeld me, and how I replide
(For this was of much length) the vild conclusion
I now begin with griefe, and shame to utter.
He would not, but by gift of my chaste body
To his concupiscible intemperate lust
Release my brother; and after much debatement,
My sisterly remorse, confutes mine honour,
And I did yeeld to him: but the next morne betimes,
His purpose surfetting, he sends a warrant
For my poore brothers head.

Duke. This is most likely.

Isab. Oh that it were as like as it is true.   (speak'st

Duk. By heaven (fond wretch) ỹ knowst not what thou
Or else thou are suborn'd against his honor
In hatefull practise: first his Integritie
Stands without blemish: next it imports no reason,
That with such vehemency he should pursue
Faults proper to himselfe: if he had so offended
He would have waigh'd thy brother by himselfe,
And not have cut him off: some one hath set you on:
Confesse the truth, and say by whose advice
Thou cam'st heere to complaine.

Isab. And is this all?

Then oh you blessed Ministers above
Keepe me in patience, and with ripened time
Unfold the evill, which is heere wrapt up
In countenance: heaven shield your Grace from woe,
As I thus wrong'd, hence unbeleeved goe.

   Duke. I know you'ld faine be gone: An Officer:
To prison with her: Shall we thus permit
A blasting and a scandalous breath to fall,
On him so neere us? This needs must be a practise;
Who knew of your intent and comming hither?

   Isa. One that I would were heere, *Frier Lodowick.*

   Duk. A ghostly Father, belike:
Who knowes that *Lodowicke*?

   Luc. My Lord, I know him, 'tis a medling Fryer,
I doe not like the man: had he been Lay my Lord,
For certaine words he spake against your Grace
In your retirment, I had swing'd him soundly.

   Duke. Words against mee? this 'a good Fryer belike
And to set on this wretched woman here
Against our Substitute: Let this Fryer be found.

   Luc. But yesternight my Lord, she and that Fryer
I saw them at the prison: a sawcy Fryar,
A very scurvy fellow.

   Peter. Blessed be your Royall Grace:
I have stood by my Lord, and I have heard
Your royall eare abus'd: first hath this woman
Most wrongfully accus'd your Substitute,
Who is as free from touch, or soyle with her
As she from one ungot.

   Duke. We did beleeve no lesse.
Know you that Frier *Lodowick* that she speakes of?

   Peter. I know him for a man divine and holy,
Not scurvy, nor a temporary medler
As he's reported by this Gentleman:
And on my trust, a man that never yet
Did (as he vouches) mis-report your Grace.

   Luc. My Lord, most villanously, beleeve it.

Peter. Well: he in time may come to cleere himselfe;
But at this instant he is sicke, my Lord:
Of a strange Feavor: upon his meere request
Being come to knowledge, that there was complaint
Intended 'gainst Lord *Angelo*, came I hether
To speake as from his mouth, what he doth know
Is true, and false: And what he with his oath
And all probation will make up full cleare
Whensoever he's convented: First for this woman,
To justifie this worthy Noble man
So vulgarly and personally accus'd,
Her shall you heare disproved to her eyes,
Till she her selfe confesse it.

   Duk. Good Frier, let's heare it:
Doe you not smile at this, Lord *Angelo*?
Oh heaven, the vanity of wretched fooles.
Give us some seates, Come cosen *Angelo*,
In this I'll be impartiall: be you Judge
Of your owne Cause: Is this the Witnes Frier?

Enter Mariana.

First let her shew your face, and after, speake.
   Mar. Pardon my Lord, I will not shew my face
Untill my husband bid me.
   Duke. What, are you married?
   Mar. No my Lord.
   Duke. Are you a Maid?
   Mar. No my Lord.
   Duk. A Widow then?
   Mar. Neither, my Lord.
   Duk. Why you are nothing then: neither Maid, Widow, nor Wife?
   Luc. My Lord, she may be a Puncke : for many of them are neither Maid, Widow, nor Wife.
   Duk. Silence that fellow: I would he had some cause to prattle for himselfe.

Luc. Well my Lord.

Mar. My Lord, I doe confesse I nere was married,
And I confesse besides, I am no Maid,
I have known my husband, yet my husband
Knowes not, that ever he knew me.

Luc. He was drunk then, my Lord, it can be no better.

Duk. For the benefit of silence, would thou wert so to.

Luc. Well, my Lord.

Duk. This is no witnesse for Lord *Angelo*.

Mar. Now I come to't, my Lord.
Shee that accuses him of Fornication,
In selfe-same manner, doth accuse my husband,
And charges him, my Lord, with such a time,
When I'le depose I had him in mine Armes
With all th'effect of Love.

Ang. Charges she moe then me?

Mar. Not that I know.

Duk. No? you say your husband.

Mar. Why just, my Lord, and that is *Angelo*,
Who thinkes he knowes, that he nere knew my body,
But knows, he thinkes, that he knowes *Isabels*.

Ang. This is a strange abuse: Let's see thy face.

Mar. My husband bids me, now I will unmaske.
This is that face, thou cruell *Angelo*
Which once thou sworst, was worth the looking on:
This is the hand, which with a vowd contract
Was fast belockt in thine: This is the body
That tooke away the match from *Isabell*,
And did supply thee at thy garden-house
In her Imagin'd person.

Duke. Know you this woman?

Luc. Carnallie she saies.

Duk. Sirha, no more.

Luc. Enough my Lord.

Ang. My Lord, I must confesse, I know this woman,
And five yeres since there was some speech of marriage
Betwixt my selfe, and her: which was broke off,

[99]

Partly for that her promis'd proportions
Came short of Composition: But in chiefe
For that her reputation was dis-valued
In levitie: Since which time of five yeres
I never spake with her, saw her, nor heard from her
Upon my faith, and honor.

    Mar. Noble Prince,
As there comes light from heaven, and words from breath,
As there is sence in truth, and truth in vertue,
I am affianced this mans wife, as strongly
As words could make up vowes: And my good Lord,
But Tuesday night last gon, in's garden house,
He knew me as a wife. As this is true,
Let me in safety raise me from my knees,
Or else for ever be confixed here
A Marble Monument.

    Ang. I did but smile till now,
Now, good my Lord, give me the scope of Justice,
My patience here is touch'd: I doe perceive
These poore informall women, are no more
But instruments of some more mightier member
That sets them on. Let me have way, my Lord
To finde this practise out.

    Duke. I, with my heart,
And punish them to your height of pleasure.
Thou foolish Frier, and thou pernicious woman
Compact with her that's gone: thinkst thou, thy oathes,
Though they would swear downe each particular Saint,
Were testimonies against his worth, and credit
That's seal'd in approbation? you, Lord *Escalus*
Sit with my Cozen, lend him your kinde paines
To finde out this abuse, whence 'tis deriv'd.
There is another Frier that set them on,
Let him be sent for.

    Peter. Would he were here, my Lord, for he indeed
Hath set the women on to this Complaint;
Your Provost knowes the place where he abides,

And he may fetch him.

Duke. Goe, doe it instantly:
And you, my noble and well-warranted Cosen
Whom it concernes to heare this matter forth,
Doe with your injuries as seemes you best
In any chastisement; I for a while
Will leave you; but stir not you till you have
Well determin'd upon these Slanderers.   *Exit.*

Esc. My Lord, wee'll doe it throughly: Signior *Lucio*, did not you say you knew that Frier *Lodowick* to be a dishonest person?

Luc. Cucullus non facit Monachum, honest in nothing but in his Clothes, and one that hath spoke most villanous speeches of the Duke.

Esc. We shall intreat you to abide heere till he come, and inforce them against him: we shall finde this Frier a notable fellow.

Luc. As any in *Vienna,* on my word.

Esc. Call that same *Isabell* here once againe. I would speake with her: pray you, my Lord, give mee leave to question, you shall see how Ile handle her.

Luc. Not better then he, by her owne report.

Esc. Say you?

Luc. Marry sir, I thinke, if you handled her privately She would sooner confesse, perchance publickely she'll be asham'd.

Enter Duke, Provost, Isabella.

Esc. I will goe darkely to worke with her.

Luc. That's the way: for women are light at midnight.

Esc. Come on Mistris, here's a Gentlewoman,
Denies all that you have said.

Luc. My Lord, here comes the rascall I spoke of,
Here, with the *Provost.*

Esc. In very good time: speake not you to him, till we call upon you.

Luc. Mum.

Esc. Come Sir, did you set these women on to slander Lord *Angelo*? they have confes'd you did.

Duk. 'Tis false.

Esc. How? Know you where you are?

Duk. Respect to your great place; and let the divell
Be sometime honour'd, for his burning throne.
Where is the *Duke*? 'tis he should heare me speake.

Esc. The *Duke's* in us: and we will heare you speake,
Looke you speake justly.

Duk. Boldly, at least. But oh poore soules,
Come you to seeke the Lamb here of the Fox;
Good night to your redresse: Is the *Duke* gone?
Then is your cause gone too: the *Duke's* unjust,
Thus to retort your manifest Appeale,
And put your triall in the villaines mouth,
Which here you come to accuse.

Luc. This is the rascall: this is he I spoke of.

Esc. Why thou unreverend, and unhallowed Fryer:
Is't not enough thou hast suborn'd these women,
To accuse this worthy man? but in foule mouth,
And in the witnesse of his proper eare,
To call him villaine; and then to glance from him,
To th'*Duke* himselfe, to taxe him with Injustice?
Take him hence; to th'racke with him: we'll towze you
Joynt by joynt, but we will know his purpose:
What? unjust?

Duk. Be not so hot: the *Duke* dare
No more stretch this finger of mine, then he
Dare racke his owne: his Subject am I not,
Nor here Provinciall: My businesse in this State
Made me a looker on here in *Vienna*,
Where I have seene corruption boyle and bubble,
Till it ore-run the Stew: Lawes, for all faults,
But faults so countenanc'd, that the strong Statutes
Stand like the forfeites in a Barbers shop,
As much in mocke, as marke.

Esc. Slander to th'State:
Away with him to prison.

Ang. What can you vouch against him Signior *Lucio*?
Is this the man that you did tell us of?

Luc. 'Tis he, my Lord: come hither goodman bald-
pate, doe you know me?

Duk. I remember you Sir, by the sound of your voice,
I met you at the Prison, in the absence of the *Duke*.

Luc. Oh, did you so? and do you remember what you
said of the *Duke*.

Duk. Most notedly Sir.

Luc. Do you so Sir: And was the *Duke* a flesh-monger, a foole, and a coward, as you then reported him
to be?

Duk. You must (Sir) change persons with me, ere you
make that my report: you indeede spoke so of him, and
much more, much worse.

Luc. Oh thou damnable fellow: did not I plucke thee
by the nose, for thy speeches?

Duk. I protest, I love the *Duke*, as I love my selfe.

Ang. Harke how the villaine would close now, after
his treasonable abuses.

Esc. Such a fellow is not to be talk'd withall: Away
with him to prison: Where is the *Provost*? away with
him to prison: lay bolts enough upon him: let him speak
no more: away with those Giglets too, and with the o-
ther confederate companion.

Duk. Stay Sir, stay a while.

Ang. What, resists he? helpe him *Lucio*.

Luc. Come sir, come sir, come sir: foh sir, why you
bald-pated lying rascall: you must be hooded must you?
show your knaves visage with a poxe to you: show your
sheepe-biting face, and be hang'd an houre: will't
not off?

Duk. Thou art the first knave, that ere mad'st a *Duke*.
First *Provost*, let me bayle these gentle three:
Sneake not away Sir, for the Fryer, and you,

Must have a word anon: lay hold on him.

Luc. This may prove worse then hanging.

Duk. What you have spoke, I pardon: sit you downe,
We'll borrow place of him; Sir, by your leave:
Ha'st thou or word, or wit, or impudence,
That yet can doe thee office? If thou ha'st
Rely upon it, till my tale be heard,
And hold no longer out.

Ang. Oh, my dread Lord,
I should be guiltier then my guiltinesse,
To thinke I can be undiscerneable,
When I perceive your grace, like powre divine,
Hath look'd upon my passes. Then good Prince,
No longer Session hold upon my shame,
But let my Triall, be mine owne Confession:
Immediate sentence then, and sequent death,
Is all the grace I beg.

Duk. Come hither *Mariana*,
Say: was't thou ere contracted to this woman?

Ang. I was my Lord.

Duk. Goe take her hence, and marry her instantly.
Doe you the office (*Fryer*) which consummate,
Returne him here againe: goe with him *Provost.* *Exit.*

Esc. My Lord, I am more amaz'd at his dishonor,
Then at the strangenesse of it.

Duk. Come hither *Isabell*,
Your *Frier* is now your Prince: As I was then
Advertysing, and holy to your businesse,
(Not changing heart with habit) I am still,
Atturnied at your service.

Isab. Oh give me pardon
That I, your vassaile, have imploid, and pain'd
Your unknowne Soveraigntie.

Duk. You are pardon'd *Isabell*:
And now, deere Maide, be you as free to us.
Your Brothers death I know sits at your heart:
And you may marvaile, why I obscur'd my selfe,

Measure, For Measure.

Labouring to save his life: and would not rather
Make rash remonstrance of my hidden powre,
Then let him so be lost: oh most kinde Maid,
It was the swift celeritie of his death,
Which I did thinke, with slower foot came on,
That brain'd my purpose: but peace be with him,
That life is better life past fearing death,
Then that which lives to feare: make it your comfort,
So happy is your Brother.

Enter Angelo, Maria, Peter, Provost.

Isab. I doe my Lord.
Duk. For this new-maried man, approaching here,
Whose salt imagination yet hath wrong'd
Your well defended honor: you must pardon
For *Mariana's* sake: But as he adjudg'd your Brother,
Being criminall, in double violation
Of sacred Chastitie, and of promise-breach,
Thereon dependant for your Brothers life,
The very mercy of the Law cries out
Most audible, even from his proper tongue.
An *Angelo* for *Claudio*, death for death:
Haste still paies haste, and leasure, answers leasure:
Like doth quit like, and *Measure* still for *Measure*:
Then *Angelo*, thy fault's thus manifested;
Which though thou would'st deny, denies thee vantage.
We doe condenme thee to the very Blocke
Where *Claudio* stoop'd to death, and with like haste.
Away with him.
Mar. Oh my most gracious Lord,
I hope you will not mocke me with a husband?
Duk. It is your husband mock't you with a husband,
Consenting to the safe-guard of your honor,
I thought your marriage fit: else Imputation,
For that he knew you, might reproach your life,
And choake your good to come: For his Possessions,
Although by confutation they are ours;

We doe en-state, and widow you with all,
To buy you a better husband.
   Mar. Oh my deere Lord,
I crave no other, nor no better man.
   Duke. Never crave him, we are definitive.
   Mar. Gentle my Liege.
   Duke. You doe but loose your labour.
Away with him to death: Now Sir, to you.
   Mar. Oh my good Lord, sweet *Isabell*, take my part,
Lend me your knees, and all my life to come,
I'll lend you all my life to doe you service.
   Duke. Against all sence you doe importune her,
Should she kneele downe, in mercie of this fact,
Her Brothers ghost, his paved bed would breake,
And take her hence in horror.
   Mar. *Isabell*:
Sweet *Isabel*, doe yet but kneele by me,
Hold up your hands, say nothing: I'll speake all.
They say best men are moulded out of faults,
And for the most, become much more the better
For being a little bad: So may my husband.
Oh *Isabel*: will you not lend a knee?
   Duke. He dies for *Claudio*'s death.
   Isab. Most bounteous Sir.
Looke if it please you, on this man condemn'd,
As if my Brother liv'd: I partly thinke,
A due sinceritie governed his deedes,
Till he did looke on me: Since it is so,
Let him not die: my Brother had but Justice,
In that he did the thing for which he dide.
For *Angelo*, his Act did not ore-take his bad intent,
And must be buried but as an intent
That perish'd by the way: thoughts are no subjects
Intents, but meerely thoughts.
   Mar. Meerely my Lord.
   Duk. Your suite's unprofitable: stand up I say:
I have bethought me of another fault.

Measure, For Measure.

Provost, how came it *Claudio* was beheaded
At an unusuall howre?

  Pro. It was commanded so.

  Duke. Had you a speciall warrant for the deed?

  Pro. No my good Lord: it was by private message.

  Duk. For which I doe discharge you of your office,
Give up your keyes.

  Pro. Pardon me, noble Lord,
I thought it was a fault, but knew it not,
Yet did repent me after more advice,
For testimony whereof, one in the prison
That should by private order else have dide,
I have reserv'd alive.

  Duk. What's he?

  Pro. His name is *Barnardine*.

  Duke. I would thou hadst done so by *Claudio*:
Goe fetch him hither, let me looke upon him.

  Esc. I am sorry, one so learned, and so wise
As you, Lord *Angelo*, have stil appear'd,
Should slip so grosselie, both in the heat of bloud
And lacke of temper'd judgement afterward.

  Ang. I am sorrie, that such sorrow I procure,
And so deepe sticks it in my penitent heart,
That I crave death more willingly then mercy,
'Tis my deserving, and I doe entreat it.

    Enter Barnardine and Provost, Claudio, Julietta.

  Duke. Which is that *Barnardine*?

  Pro. This my Lord.

  Duke. There was a Friar told me of this man.
Sirha, thou art said to have a stubborne soule
That apprehends no further then this world,
And squar'st thy life according: Thou'rt condemn'd,
But for those earthly faults, I quit them all,
And pray thee take this mercie to provide
For better times to come: Frier advise him.
I leave him to your hand. What muffeld fellow's that?

[107]

Pro. This is another prisoner that I sav'd,
Who should have di'd when *Claudio* lost his head,
As like almost to *Claudio*, as himselfe.

Duke. If he be like your brother, for his sake
Is he pardon'd, and for your lovelie sake
Give me your hand, and say you will be mine,
He is my brother too: But fitter time for that:
By this Lord *Angelo* perceives he's safe,
Methinkes I see a quickning in his eye:
Well *Angelo*, your evill quits you well.
Looke that you love your wife: her worth, worth yours
I finde an apt remission in my selfe:
And yet heere's one in place I cannot pardon,
You sirha, that knew me for a foole, a Coward,
One all of Luxurie, an asse, a mad man:
Wherein have I so deserv'd of you
That you extoll me thus?

Luc. 'Faith my Lord, I spoke it but according to the
trick: if you will hang me for it you may: but I had rather it would please you, I might be whipt.

Duke. Whipt first, sir, and hang'd after.
Proclaime it Provost round about the Citie,
If any woman wrong'd by this lewd fellow
(As I have heard him sweare himselfe there's one
whom he begot with childe) let her appeare,
And he shall marry her: the nuptiall finish'd,
Let him be whipt and hang'd.

Luc. I beseech your Highnesse doe not marry me to
a Whore: your Highnesse said even now I made you a
Duke, good my Lord do not recompence me, in making
me a Cuckold.

Duke. Upon mine honor thou shalt marrie her.
Thy slanders I forgive, and therewithall
Remit thy other forfeits: take him to prison,
And see our pleasure herein executed.

Luc. Marrying a punke my Lord, is pressing to death,
Whipping and hanging.

Duke. Slandering a Prince deserves it.
She *Claudio* that you wrong'd, looke you restore.
Joy to you *Mariana*, love her *Angelo*:
I have confes'd her, and I know her vertue.
Thanks good friend, *Escalus*, for thy much goodnesse,
There's more behinde that is more gratulate.
Thanks *Provost* for thy care, and secrecie,
We shall imploy thee in a worthier place.
Forgive him *Angelo*, that brought you home
The head of *Ragozine* for *Claudio's*,
Th'offence pardons it selfe. Deere *Isabell*
I have a motion much imports your good,
Whereto if you'll a willing eare incline;
What's mine is yours, and what is yours is mine.
So bring us to our Pallace, where wee'll show
What's yet behinde, that meete you all should know.

The Scene Vienna.

The names of all the Actors.

Vincentio: the Duke.
Angelo, the Deputie.
Escalus, an ancient Lord.
Claudio, a yong Gentleman.
Lucio, a fantastique.
2.Other like Gentlemen.
Provost.
Thomas.
Peter. } *2. Friers.*
Elbow, a simple Constable.
Froth, a foolish Gentleman.
Clowne.
Abhorson, an Executioner.
Barnardine, a dissolute prisoner.

Measure, For Measure.

Isabella, sister to Claudio.
Mariana, betrothed to Angelo.
Juliet, beloved of Claudio.
Francisca, a Nun.
Mistris Over-don, a Bawd.

FINIS.

Endnotes

Page 27
   warpe: deviate.

Page 28
   waste / Thy selfe upon thy vertues: an allusion to the parable of the Talents (Matthew 25:14–30).

   tonch'd: compositorial error for 'touch'd'.

Page 29
   Aves: shouts of greeting.

   Exit.: this is a misplaced direction for the Duke, who exits after the next line; the text contains numerous other errors in the placement of exit directions.

Page 30
   King of Hungary: a much disputed allusion, possibly to King James's peace negotiations from 1603 to 1604 with European monarchs.

   I, that he raz'd: here and elsewhere 'I' is a variant spelling of 'aye'.

   rallish: relish.

   List: border or edge of a cloth, usually of an inferior material from the body of the cloth, in this case velvet.

   three pild-peece: having a heavy nap or pile, with a pun on 'pild' here and in the following lines as 'infected with venereal disease'.

Page 31
   Kersey: coarse cloth, with a pun on 'homely'.

   Madam Mitigation: he puns on her ability to 'mitigate' sexual desire.

   Dollours: pun on 'dollars', the English term for German and Spanish coins.

Endnotes

French crowne: coin, with pun on baldness caused by the 'French', i.e. venereal, disease.

figuring: portraying.

Ciatica: sciatica, a nerve disorder.

Page 32

sweat: sweating sickness, or, possibly, treatment for venereal disease.

Custom-shrunke: losing customers.

Groping for Trowts, in a peculiar River: slang for 'having sexual intercourse with a forbidden woman'.

maid with child: here she uses the word 'maid' to mean 'unmarried woman', but the Clown takes the word to mean 'virgin' and responds 'woman with maid', i.e., a woman pregnant with a female child.

howses: brothels.

stand for seed: lie fallow.

Burger: middle-class citizen or businessman.

Page 33

Rats that rauyn downe their proper bane: 'bane' is poison, here with a pun on 'ratsbane,' a poisonous plant, suggesting that the rats 'ravin' or devour their own poison.

Page 34

denunciation: public announcement.

outward Order: i.e., marriage ceremony.

propogation of a Dowre: production of a dowry.

un-scowr'd: unpolished, hence rusty.

Zodiacks: years.

Page 35

prone: inclined to good, hence provoking mercy.

speechlesse: expressive or persuasive without speech.

Page 37

precise: overly strict.

Sisterstood: error, probably compositorial, for 'sisterhood'.

steed: stead, direct.

Page 38

Lapwing: bird known for luring another astray.

fewnes: a few words.

seednes: action of sowing.

teemiug: compositorial error for 'teeming'.

snow-broth: melted snow.

Page 39

rebate: reduce.

Page 41

Goe to: get to the point.

Page 42

out at Elbow: in clothing with worn-out sleeves, hence foolish.

parcell: part-time.

hot-house: bathing house, slang for 'brothel', which Elbow does not recognise.

detest: Elbow's error for 'respect'.

Cardinally: Elbow's error for 'carnally'.

honorable: Elbow's error for 'dishonorable'.

stewd prewyns: prunes were a favourite dish of the 'stews' or brothels and are slang for 'prostitutes'.

Page 43

Hallowmas: 1 November, All Saints' Day.

Allhallond-Eve: 31 October, Halloween.

Page 44

nothing done to her once: Pompey puns on 'done' as meaning 'have sexual intercourse with'.

supposd: Pompey's error for 'deposed'.

Endnotes

respected: Elbow's error for 'suspected'.

Hanniball: Elbow's error for 'cannibal', with an unintended pun on the other famous general, Pompey.

Page 45
draw you: entice to crime, with a pun on 'draw the tap,' i.e. serve ale.

Page 46
bum: buttocks.

drabs: prostitutes.

knaves: base fellows.

heading: beheading, also used in this scene to pun on 'taking maiden-heads' or deflowering.

Carman whip his Jade: cart driver whip his horse (jade).

Page 47
men in your Ward: other watchmen.

Page 49
Cipher of a Function: symbol of 'no value by itself but which increases or decreases the value of other figures according to its position' (*OED*).

Page 50
of season: in season.

Page 51
di'd: died.

gaule: vex, oppress.

pelting: paltry.

Page 53
'Save your Honour: God save your Honour (Isabella and Lucio exit after this line).

Violet in the Sunne: the violet is a symbol of purity.

womans lightnesse: woman's promiscuity.

[114]

Endnotes

Page 55
Benedicite: Bless you.

onely: only.

with boote: with advantage.

Page 57
Let be: Let me be.

en-shield: shielded.

Page 58
ignomie in ransome: ignominy in ransom, hence ransom purchased from shame or dishonour.

Page 59
fedarie: accomplice.

glasses: mirrors.

destin'd Liverie: i.e. act like a woman and not like a nun.

Page 60
reporr: error, probably compositorial, for 'report'.

prolixious: long in duration.

approofe: approval.

prompture: prompting.

"More . . . Chastitie: although this line lacks the closing quotation mark, the opening quotation mark suggests that the line is an adage or a prepared remark that Isabella will repeat to Claudio.

Page 61
Sapego: serpigo, a skin disease.

Page 62
palsied-Eld: palsied elders.

moe: more.

Leiger: resident.

Page 63
Perpetuall durance: life imprisonment.

[115]

Endnotes

emmew: enclose; possibly a compositorial error for 'enew,' i.e. to drive into water.

prenzie: word of unknown meaning, probably akin to 'falsely rich' or 'pure'.

Page 64
prenzie gardes: false trimmings.

fin'de: fined.

kneaded clod: lump of earth.

recide: reside.

Page 67
combynate-husband: husband by contract.

onely: only.

Page 68
steed up: keep.

scaled: properly weighed.

bastard: sweetened wine, with a pun on 'illegitimate children of mixed race'.

Page 69
two usuries: the first is fornication, now outlawed, and the second is money-lending.

facing: boasting, with a pun on the 'facing', or inner edge, of the furred gown.

cram a maw: stuff a stomach.

Page 70
Cord: the friar's waist cord, with a pun on 'hangman's rope'.

Pigmalions Images: in Greek myth, Pygmalion created a perfect woman from a statue, and this myth was often treated bawdily in the Renaissance.

Trot: slang for 'hag' or 'prostitute'.

in the tub: taking the cure for venereal disease.

unshun'd: inevitable.

Endnotes

  crabbed: disagreeable.

  extirpe: root up.

  motion generative: sexless puppet.

  Cod-peece: slang for 'male genitals'.

Page 72
  put a ducket in her Clack-dish: literally, put a coin in a beggar's dish, with pun on 'have intercourse with'.

  Crochets: peculiar or perverse whims.

  wise: Lucio appears to use the word to mean 'cunning', while the Duke takes it to mean 'prudent' or 'learned'.

Page 73
  Tunne-dish: funnel used in brewing ale, here slang for 'have sexual intercourse'.

  ungenitur'd: sexless.

  eeves: eaves.

  untrussing: undressing.

  eate Mutton on Fridaies: eat meat on Fridays, religious fast-days, with a pun on 'mutton' as 'whore'.

  mouth with: kiss.

  smelt: smelled of.

  scape: escape.

Page 74
  Philip and Jacob: 1 May, the feast day of the two saints; also May Day, a feast of merriment and sexual licence.

Page 77
  planched: made of planks.

Page 79
  snatches: quibbles.

  Gyves: shackles.

Endnotes

Abhorson: his name puns on 'abhorred one' and 'son of a whore'.

Page 80
Painting: wearing heavy makeup.

y'are: yare, i.e. prepared.

Page 81
meal'd: stained.

sildome: seldom.

unsisting: word of uncertain meaning, possibly a negative form of 'sist', to stop or stay.

Posterne: back gate or door.

Page 83
undoubtfull: certain.

wreaklesse: reckless.

Page 84
bar'de: bared.

Page 85
M' Rash . . . stabb'd Pots: Pompey introduces a number of puns here on the types of young men now in the prison.

Page 89
Covent: religious community.

Wend: go.

Page 90
woodman: huntsman, with a pun on 'woman-hunter'.

Medler: slang for 'prostitute'.

Page 91
reliver: give back.

ou rathorities: compositorial error for 'our authorities'.

Page 92
blench: flinch.

Endnotes

Page 93
   hent: reached.

   razure: erasure.

Page 95
   caracts: signs.

Page 96
   refeld: refuted, refused.

Page 97
   Lay: non-clerical.

   swing'd: past tense of 'swinge', to beat.

   ungot: unbegotten.

Page 98
   Are you a Maid?: Are you unmarried, i.e. a virgin?

   Puncke: prostitute.

Page 99
   known my husband: had sexual intercourse with my husband.

   moe: more (other) men.

Page 101
   Cucullus non facit Monachum: the hood does not make the monk (Latin: proverbial).

   light: promiscuous.

Page 102
   towze: push or drag about.

Page 103
   flesh-monger: fornicator.

   Giglets: lewd women.

   sheepe-biting: thieving.

   mad'st a Duke: Lucio has pulled off the Duke's hood and he is now recognisable.

Endnotes

Page 104
>   *dread*: dreaded.

>   *Session*: official assembly.

>   *Exit*: this is an exit marker for Angelo, Mariana and Friar Peter.

>   *Atturnied*: attornied.

Page 105
>   *salt*: lecherous.

>   *Measure still for Measure*: an allusion to Matthew 7.1–2, 'Judge not, that ye be not judged. For with what judgement ye judge, ye shal be judged, and with what measure ye mette, it shall be measured to you againe.'

>   *confutation*: action of disproving.

Page 106
>   *paved bed*: tomb covered with paving stones.

Page 108
>   *di'd*: died.

>   *quickning*: restoration of life.

Page 109
>   *gratulate*: pleasing or worthy of congratulations.

Appendix

MEASVRE,
For Measure.

Actus primus, Scena prima.

Enter Duke, Escalus, Lords.

Duke.

Esc. My Lord.

Duk. Of Gouernment, the properties to vn- (fold,
Would seeme in me t'affect speech & discourse,
Since I am put to know, that your owne Science
Exceedes (in that) the lists of all aduice
My strength can giue you: Then no more remaines
But that, to your sufficiency, as your worth is able,
And let them worke: The nature of our People,
Our *Cities Institutions*, and the Termes
For Common Iustice, y'are as pregnant in
As Art, and practise, hath inriched any
That we remember: There is our Commission,
From which, we would not haue you warpe; call hither,
I say, bid come before vs *Angelo*:
What figure of vs thinke you, he will beare.
For you must know, we haue with speciall soule
Elected him our absence to supply;
Lent him our terror, drest him with our loue,
And giuen his Deputation all the Organs
Of our owne powre: What thinke you of it?

Esc. If any in *Vienna* be of worth
To vndergoe such ample grace, and honour,
It is Lord *Angelo*.

Enter Angelo.

Duk. Looke where he comes.

Ang. Alwayes obedient to your Graces will,
I come to know your pleasure.

Duke. Angelo:
There is a kinde of Character in thy life,
That to th'obseruer, doth thy history
Fully vnfold: Thy selfe, and thy belongings
Are not thine owne so proper, as to waste
Thy selfe vpon thy vertues; they on thee:
Heauen doth with vs, as we, with Torches doe,
Not light them for themselues: For if our vertues
Did not goe forth of vs, 'twere all alike
As if we had them not: Spirits are not finely touch'd,
But to fine issues: nor nature neuer lends
The smallest scruple of her excellence,
But like a thrifty goddesse, she determines
Her selfe the glory of a creditour,
Both thankes, and vse; but I do bend my speech

To one that can my part in him aduertise;
Hold therefore *Angelo*:
In our remoue, be thou at full, our selfe:
Mortallitie and Mercie in *Vienna*
Liue in thy tongue, and heart: Old *Escalus*
Though first in question, is thy secondary.
Take thy Commission.

Ang. Now good my Lord
Let there be some more test, made of my mettle,
Before so noble, and so great a figure
Be stamp't vpon it.

Duk. No more euasion:
We haue with a leauen'd, and prepared choice
Proceeded to you; therefore take your honors:
Our haste from hence is of so quicke condition,
That it prefers it selfe, and leaues vnquestion'd
Matters of needfull value: We shall write to you
As time, and our concernings shall importune,
How it goes with vs, and doe looke to know
What doth befall you here. So fare you well:
To th'hopefull execution doe I leaue you,
Of your Commissions.

Ang. Yet giue leaue (my Lord,)
That we may bring you something on the way.

Duk. My haste may not admit it,
Nor neede you (on mine honor) haue to doe
With any scruple: your scope is as mine owne,
So to inforce, or qualifie the Lawes
As to your soule seemes good: Giue me your hand,
Ile priuily away: I loue the people,
But doe not like to stage me to their eyes:
Though it doe well, I doe not rellish well
Their lowd applause, and Aues vehement:
Nor doe I thinke the man of safe discretion
That do's affect it. Once more fare you well.

Ang. The heauens giue safety to your purposes.

Esc. Lead forth, and bring you backe in happi-
nesse.   *Exit.*

Duk. I thanke you, fare you well.

Esc. I shall desire you, Sir, to giue me leaue
To haue free speech with you; and it concernes me
To looke into the bottome of my place:
A powre I haue, but of what strength and nature,
I am not yet instructed.

Ang. 'Tis so with me: Let vs with-draw together,
And we may soone our satisfaction haue
Touching that point.

Esc. Ile wait vpon your honor.   *Exeunt.*

F   *Scena*

Scena Secunda.

Enter Lucio, and two other Gentlemen.

Luc. If the Duke, with the other Dukes, come not to composition with the King of Hungary, why then all the Dukes fall vpon the King.

1.Gent. Heauen grant vs its peace, but not the King of Hungaries.

2.Gent. Amen.

Luc. Thou conclud'st like the Sanctimonious Pirat, that went to sea with the ten Commandements, but scrap'd one out of the Table.

2.Gent. Thou shalt not Steale?

Luc. I, that he raz'd.

1.Gent. Why? 'twas a commandement, to command the Captaine and all the rest from their functions: they put forth to steale: There's not a Souldier of vs all, that in the thankf-giuing before meate, do rallish the petition well, that praies for peace.

2.Gent. I neuer heard any Souldier dislike it.

Luc. I beleeue thee: for I thinke thou neuer was't where Grace was said.

2.Gent. No? a dozen times at least.

1.Gent. What? In meeter?

Luc. In any proportion: or in any language.

1.Gent. I thinke, or in any Religion.

Luc. I, why not? Grace, is Grace, despight of all controuersie: as for example; Thou thy selfe art a wicked villaine, despight of all Grace.

1.Gent. Well: there went but a paire of sheeres betweene vs.

Luc. I grant: as there may betweene the Lists, and the Veluet. Thou art the List.

1.Gent. And thou the Veluet; thou art good veluet; thou'rt a three pild-peece I warrant thee: I had as liefe be a Lyst of an English Kersey, as be pil'd, as thou art pil'd, for a French Veluet. Do I speake feelingly now?

Luc. I thinke thou do'st: and indeed with most painfull feeling of thy speech: I will, out of thine owne confession, learne to begin thy health; but, whilst I liue forget to drinke after thee.

1.Gen. I think I haue done my selfe wrong, haue I not?

2.Gent. Yes, that thou hast; whether thou art tainted, or free. *Enter Bawde.*

Luc. Behold, behold, where Madam *Mitigation* comes. I haue purchas'd as many diseases vnder her Roofe, As come to

2.Gent. To what, I pray?

Luc. Iudge.

2.Gent. To three thousand Dollours a yeare.

1.Gent. I, and more.

Luc. A French crowne more.

1.Gent. Thou art alwayes figuring diseases in me; but thou art full of error, I am sound.

Luc. Nay, not (as one would say) healthy: but so sound, as things that are hollow; thy bones are hollow; Impiety has made a feast of thee.

1.Gent. How now, which of your hips has the most profound Ciatica?

Bawd. Well, well: there's one yonder arrested, and carried to prison, was worth fiue thousand of you all.

2.Gent. Who's that I pray'thee?

Bawd. Marry Sir, that's *Claudio,* Signior *Claudio.*

1.Gent. *Claudio* to prison? 'tis not so.

Bawd. Nay, but I know 'tis so: I saw him arrested: saw him carried away: and which is more, within these three daies his head to be chop'd off.

Luc. But, after all this fooling, I would not haue it so: Art thou sure of this?

Bawd. I am too sure of it: and it is for getting Madam *Iulietta* with childe.

Luc. Beleeue me this may be: he promis'd to meete me two howres since, and he was euer precise in promise keeping.

2.Gent. Besides you know, it drawes somthing neere to the speech we had to such a purpose.

1.Gent. But most of all agreeing with the proclamatiõ.

Luc. Away: let's goe learne the truth of it. *Exit.*

Bawd. Thus, what with the war; what with the sweat, what with the gallowes, and what with pouerty, I am Custom-shrunke. How now? what's the newes with you. *Enter Clowne.*

Clo. Yonder man is carried to prison.

Baw. Well: what has he done?

Clo. A Woman.

Baw. But what's his offence?

Clo. Groping for Trowts, in a peculiar Riuer.

Baw. What? is there a maid with child by him?

Clo. No: but there's a woman with maid by him: you haue not heard of the proclamation, haue you?

Baw. What proclamation, man?

Clow. All howses in the Suburbs of *Vienna* must bee pluck'd downe.

Bawd. And what shall become of those in the Citie?

Clow. They shall stand for seed: they had gon downe to, but that a wise Burger put in for them.

Bawd. But shall all our houses of resort in the Suburbs be puld downe?

Clow. To the ground, Mistris.

Bawd. Why heere's a change indeed in the Commonwealth: what shall become of me?

Clow. Come: feare not you: good Counsellors lacke no Clients: though you change your place, you neede not change your Trade: Ile bee your Tapster still; courage, there will bee pitty taken on you; you that haue worne your eyes almost out in the seruice, you will bee considered.

Bawd. What's to doe heere, *Thomas* Tapster? let's withdraw?

Clo. Here comes Signior *Claudio,* led by the Prouost to prison: and there's Madam *Iuliet.* *Exeunt.*

Scena Tertia.

Enter Prouost, Claudio, Iuliet, Officers, Lucio & 2.Gent.

Cla. Fellow, why do'st thou show me thus to th'world? Beare me to prison, where I am committed.

Pro. I do it not in euill disposition, But from Lord *Angelo* by speciall charge.

Clau. Thus can the demy-god (Authority) Make vs pay downe, for our offence, by waight The words of heauen: on whom it will, it will, On whom it will not (foe) yet still 'tis iust. (straint.

Luc. Why how now? how is't whence comes this re-

Cla. From too much liberty, (my *Lucio*) Liberty As surfet is the father of much fast, So euery Scope by the immoderate vse Turnes to restraint: Our Natures doe pursue

Like

Like Rats that rauyn downe their proper Bane,
A thirfty euill, and when we drinke; we die.

Luc. If I could fpeake fo wifely vnder an arreft, I
would fend for certaine of my Creditors : and yet, to fay
the truth, I had as liefhaue the foppery of freedome, as
the mortality of imprifonment : what's thy offence,
Claudio ?

Cla. What (but to fpeake of) would offend againe.

Luc. What, is't murder?

Cla. No.

Luc. Lecherie?

Cla. Call it fo;

Pro. Away, Sir, you muft goe.

Cla. One word, good friend :

Lucio, a word with you.

Luc. A hundred :

If they'll doe you any good : Is *Lechery* fo look'd after ?

Cla. Thus ftands it with me : vpon a true contract
I got poffeffion of *Iulietas* bed,
You know the Lady, fhe is faft my wife,
Saue that we doe the denunciation lacke
Of outward Order. This we came not to,
Onely for propagation of a Dowre
Remaining in the Coffer of her friends,
From whom we thought it meet to hide our Loue
Till Time had made them for vs. But it chances
The ftealth of our moft mutuall entertainment
With Charactter too groffe, is writ on *Iuliet.*

Luc. With childe, perhaps ?

Cla. Vnhappely, euen fo.
And the new Deputie, now for the Duke,
Whether it be the fault and glimpfe of newnes,
Or whether that the body publique, be
A horfe whereon the Gouernor doth ride,
Who newly in the Seate, that it may know
He can command; lets it ftrait feele the fpur :
Whether the Tirranny be in his place,
Or in his Eminence that fills it vp
I ftagger in : but this new Gouernor
Awakes me all the inrolled penalties
Which haue (like vn-fcowr'd Armor) hung by th'wall
So long, that nineteene Zodiacks haue gone round,
And none of them beene worne; and for a name
Now puts the drowfie and neglected Act
Frefhly on me: 'tis furely for a name.

Luc. I warrant it is : And thy head ftands fo tickle on
thy fhoulders, that a milke-maid, if fhe be in loue, may
figh it off : Send after the Duke, and appeale to him.

Cla. I haue done fo, but hee's not to be found.
I pre'thee (*Lucio*) doe mee this kinde feruice :
This day, my fifter fhould the Cloyfter enter,
And there receiue her approbation.
Acquaint her with the danger of my ftate,
Implore her, in my voice, that fhe make-friends
To the ftrict deputie : bid her felfe affay him,
I haue great hope in that : for in her youth
There is a prone and fpeechleffe dialect,
Such as moue men : befides, fhe hath profperous Art
When fhe will play with reafon, and difcourfe,
And well fhe can perfwade.

Luc. I pray fhee may ; afwell for the encouragement
of the like, which elfe would ftand vnder greeuous im-
pofition : as for the enioying of thy life, who I would be
forry fhould bee thus foolifhly loft, at a game of ticke-
tacke : Ile to her.

Cla. I thinke you good friend *Lucio.*

Luc. Within two houres.

Cla. Come Officer, away.   *Exeunt.*

Scena Quarta.

Enter Duke and Frier Thomas.

Duk. No : holy Father, throw away that thought,
Beleeue not that the dribling dart of Loue
Can pierce a compleat bofome : why, I defire thee
To giue me fecret harbour, hath a purpofe
More graue, and wrinkled, then the aimes, and ends
Of burning youth.

Fri. May your Grace fpeake of it ?

Duk. My holy Sir, none better knowes then you
How I haue euer lou'd the life remoued
And held in idle price, to haunt affemblies
Where youth, and coft, witleffe brauery keepes.
I haue deliuer'd to Lord *Angelo*
(A man of ftricture and firme abftinence)
My abfolute power, and place here in *Vienna*,
And he fuppofes me trauaild to *Poland*,
(For fo I haue ftrewd it in the common eare)
And fo it is receiu'd : Now (pious Sir)
You will demand of me, why I do this.

Fri. Gladly, my Lord.

Duk. We haue ftrict Statutes, and moft biting Lawes,
(The needfull bits and curbes to headftrong weedes,)
Which for this fourteene yeares, we haue let flip,
Euen like an ore-growne Lyon in a Caue
That goes not out to prey : Now, as fond Fathers,
Hauing bound vp the threatning twigs of birch,
Onely to ftick it in their childrens fight,
For terror, not to vfe : in time the rod
More mock'd, then fear'd : fo our Decrees,
Dead to infliction, to themfelues are dead,
And libertie, plucks Iuftice by the nofe ;
The Baby beates the Nurfe, and quite athwart
Goes all decorum.

Fri. It refted in your Grace
To vnloofe this tyde-vp Iuftice, when you pleaf'd :
And it in you more dreadfull would haue feem'd
Then in Lord *Angelo.*

Duk. I doe feare : too dreadfull :
Sith 'twas my fault, to giue the people fcope,
'T would be my tirrany to ftrike and gall them,
For what I bid them doe : For, we bid this be done
When euill deedes haue their permiffiue paffe,
And not the punifhment : therefore indeede (my father)
I haue on *Angelo* impos'd the office,
Who may in th'ambufh of my name, ftrike home,
And yet, my nature neuer in the fight
To do in flander : And to behold his fway
I will, as 'twere a brother of your Order,
Vifit both Prince, and People : Therefore I pre'thee
Supply me with the habit, and inftruct me
How I may formally in perfon beare
Like a true *Frier* : Moe reafons for this action
At our more leyfure, fhall I render you ;
Onely, this one : Lord *Angelo* is precife,
Stands at a guard with Enuie : fcarce confeffes
That his blood flowes : or that his appetite
Is more to bread then ftone : hence fhall we fee
If power change purpofe : what our Seemers be. *Exit.*

F 2   *Scena*

Scena Quinta.

Enter Isabell and Francisca a Nun.

Isa. And haue you Nuns no farther priuiledges?
Nun. Are not these large enough?
Isa. Yes truely; I speake not as desiring more,
But rather wishing a more strict restraint
Vpon the Sisterstood, the Votarists of Saint *Clare.*
                    Lucio within.
Luc. Hoa? peace be in this place.
Isa. Who's that which cals?
Nun. It is a mans voice: gentle *Isabella*
Turne you the key, and know his businesse of him;
You may; I may not: you are yet vnsworne:
When you haue vowd, you must not speake with men,
But in the presence of the *Prioresse*;
Then if you speake, you must not show your face;
Or if you show your face, you must not speake:
He cals againe: I pray you answere him.
Isa. Peace and prosperitie: who is't that cals?
Luc. Haile Virgin, (if you be) as those cheeke-Roses
Proclaime you are no lesse: can you so steed me,
As bring me to the sight of *Isabella,*
A Nouice of this place, and the faire Sister
To her vnhappie brother *Claudio*?
Isa. Why her vnhappy Brother? Let me aske,
The rather for I now must make you know
I am that *Isabella,* and his Sister.
Luc. Gentle & faire: your Brother kindly greets you;
Not to be weary with you; he's in prison.
Isa. Woe me; for what?
Luc. For that, which if my selfe might be his Iudge,
He should receiue his punishment, in thankes:
He hath got his friend with childe.
Isa. Sir, make me not your storie.
Luc. 'Tis true; I would not, though 'tis my familiar sin,
With Maids to seeme the Lapwing, and to iest
Tongue, far from heart: play with all Virgins so:
I hold you as a thing en-skied, and sainted,
By your renouncement, an immortall spirit
And to be talk'd with in sincerity,
As with a Saint.
Isa. You doe blaspheme the good, in mocking me.
Luc. Doe not beleeue it: sewnes, and truth; tis thus,
Your brother, and his louer haue embrac'd;
As those that feed, grow full: as blossoming Time
That from the seednes, the bare fallow brings
To teeming foyson: euen so her plenteous wombe
Expresseth his full Tilth, and husbandry.
Isa. Some one with childe by him? my cosen *Iuliet*?
Luc. Is she your cosen?
Isa. Adoptedly, as schoole-maids change their names
By vaine, though apt affection.
Luc. She it is.
Isa. Oh, let him marry her.
Luc. This is the point.
The Duke is very strangely gone from hence;
Bore many gentlemen (my selfe being one)
In hand, and hope of action: but we doe learne,
By those that know the very Nerues of State,
His giuing-out, were of an infinite distance
From his true meant designe: vpon his place,

(And with full line of his authority)
Gouernes Lord *Angelo*; A man, whose blood
Is very snow-broth: one, who neuer feeles
The wanton stings, and motions of the sence;
But doth rebate, and blunt his naturall edge
With profits of the minde: Studie, and fast
He (to giue feare to vse, and libertie,
Which haue, for long, run by the hideous law,
As Myce, by Lyons) hath pickt out an act,
Vnder whose heauy sence, your brothers life
Fals into forfeit: he arrests him on it,
And followes close the rigor of the Statute
To make him an example: all hope is gone,
Vnlesse you haue the grace, by your faire praier
To soften *Angelo*: And that's my pith of businesse
'Twixt you, and your poore brother.
Isa. Doth he so,
Seeke his life?
Luc. Has censur'd him already;
And as I heare, the Prouost hath a warrant
For's execution.
Isa. Alas: what poore
Abilitie's in me, to doe him good.
Luc. Assay the powre you haue.
Isa. My power? alas, I doubt.
Luc. Our doubts are traitors
And makes vs loose the good we oft might win,
By fearing to attempt: Goe to Lord *Angelo*
And let him learne to know, when Maidens sue
Men giue like gods: but when they weepe and kneele,
All their petitions, are as freely theirs
As they themselues would owe them.
Isa. Ile see what I can doe.
Luc. But speedily.
Isa. I will about it strait;
No longer staying, but to giue the Mother
Notice of my affaire: I humbly thanke you:
Commend me to my brother: soone at night
Ile send him certaine word of my successe.
Luc. I take my leaue of you.
Isa. Good sir, adieu.   *Exeunt.*

Actus Secundus. Scœna Prima.

Enter Angelo, Escalus, and seruants, Iustice.

Ang. We must not make a scar-crow of the Law,
Setting it vp to feare the Birds of prey,
And let it keepe one shape, till custome make it
Their pearch, and not their terror.
Esc. I, but yet
Let vs be keene, and rather cut a little
Then fall, and bruise to death: alas, this gentleman
Whom I would saue, had a most noble father,
Let but your honour know
(Whom I beleeue to be most strait in vertue)
That in the working of your owne affections,
Had time coherd with Place, or place with wishing,
Or that the resolute acting of our blood
Could haue attaind th'effect of your owne purpose,
Whether you had not sometime in your life
Er'd in this point, which now you censure him,
And puld the Law vpon you.
Ang. 'Tis one thing to be tempted (*Escalus*)
                                            Another